Winter Tales II
Women on the Art of Aging

Winter Tales II
Women on the Art of Aging

edited by

R.A. Rycraft
and
Leslie What

SERVING HOUSE BOOKS

Winter Tales II: Women on the Art of Aging

ISBN: 978-0-9838289-6-9

Cover photo: Kelsi Kessler

Serving House Books logo by Barry Lereng Wilmont

Published by Serving House Books, LLC
Copenhagen, Denmark and Florham Park, NJ

www.servinghousebooks.com

First Serving House Books Edition 2012

For Our Moms:

Patricia Ann Rycraft
and
Hannah Nelson

For Wayne —
Couldn't have
done this without
the stuff I learned
from you —)
Thanks!
— Diane

The Moving Finger writes; and having writ, / Moves on . . .
—Edward FitzGerald, *The Rubáiyát of Omar Khayyám*

*I could not, at any age, be content to take my place in
a corner by the fireside and simply look on.*
—Eleanor Roosevelt

Table of Contents

Winter Tales II
Women on the Art of Aging
An Introduction

We're all in this together. This aging thing. This becoming. Sisterhood of the Suddenly Senior. For some, it is an uncomfortable awareness of the mortality of *self.* For many others, though, it is the first comfortable embrace since adolescence of *self.*

Consider the experiences we share, experiences that pester our bodies, our minds. Achy knees and hips, perhaps arthritic, perhaps requiring replacements. Cracking teeth. Thinning hair. The whole menopausal matron thing: the gaining, the shifting, the shrinking, the spreading, the drooping. The sweltering hot flashes, sleepless nights, and erratic libido. The whisker growing and plucking in all of its various forms: the black, the gray, the always wiry, the soft white curly strands that grow undetected on a lower cheek until one day when the light is just right—probably in the car and far removed from a pair of tweezers—you look in the mirror and it's there, winding its way down your jaw.

There is the forgetfulness, like recalling people's names, remembering the location of keys, cell phones, or the name of the movie watched on TV last night. There are more doctor visits. More prescriptions for high blood pressure, high cholesterol, high anxiety, and low hormone levels. The dreaded mammograms and colonoscopies. The diagnoses. The inevitability of change and loss. People—loved ones—departing. And we left only with whimsical memory to keep them alive within us.

Thankfully, loss isn't the only inevitability. People inhabit our worlds in expected and unexpected ways, whether it is the birth of kids or grandkids, the discovery of friends and loves, new and old. People—real and unreal—are found in the characters that fill our television, movie, and computer screens. They are found in the characters that *people* books, like this one. In these pages, you will meet real women dealing with adjustments in their lives similar to your own and, hopefully, find comfort in the fact that you are part of a large sisterhood of aging women, many of whom seem to speak for you, your experiences mirrored in theirs.

Meet Kelly Cherry, Poet Laureate of Virginia, who writes about the ephemeral nature of companionship as well as the sense of possibilities lost with each passing birthday. Ursula K. Le Guin discusses how long it takes to become "human." Dorianne Laux's poetry illuminates how "the future shows up everywhere." Ellen Visson walks us through the process of accepting our aging selves: "O Woe Is Me . . . and There You Meta-Have it." Laurie Stone talks about embracing love and relocating her East Coast life to Phoenix, Arizona. Molly Giles wonders where all the old ladies have gone. And Gladys Swan offers a nostalgic reflection into her childhood—"Oh my, that happened sixty-odd years ago"—coming to the conclusion that the experiences of a lifetime lead to "original authenticity."

Original authenticity is revealed in the essays of Abby Frucht and Supriya Bhatnagar, who write about self-knowledge gained through the scars of inescapable loss, and Valerie Miner, who writes of her activism and treks to unknown places, adventures that shaped the woman she is today. Alexandra Marshall's journey brought her to the understanding that self—like dance—evolves in "phrases of movement." Elisabeth Murawski attempts to reconcile the internalized image of self "trapped in flesh that sags like yesterday's balloon," while Bette Lynch Husted sees herself as the *girl* "dancing still in these bones." Then there is Roisin McLean who appraises her nude, sixty-year-old body, pondering loneliness and what she wants out of life, post divorce, only to discover that to "smell the coffee, rich, mellow, and round" is to experience a modicum of peace. And Susan M. Tiberghien comes to an awareness we can all appreciate— those who followed her into this life taught her the immortality of love.

You'll discover that the women of *Winter Tales II* do not buy into the idea that aging and beauty are mutually exclusive. Wait until you see Fax Sinclair's portraits of "Mardi Gras," "Cindy & Billy," "Muzza Love," and "Sixty." Michelle Bitting challenges women, "dumbstruck in their L'Oréal lips and pastel sweaters," to reconsider conventional ideas about beauty. Artisan Diane McWhorter talks about being self-employed, and says, "I won't be able to do this as long as I will need to." We poke fun at ourselves, too. Jan Eliot's comic strips— such as "No Offense, Mom" and "Well Seasoned"—are sure to make you laugh and think, "Yeah, I *know* that." Comedienne Leigh Anne Jasheway chronicles a hilarious visit to an "aesthetic surgeon" and compares her unmoisturized face to a "distressed" piece of furniture.

Reflections on mortality are present, too—at times sad, but always honest and approached straight-on, holding no punches. Renée Ashley muses on the eighty-year-old woman her mother is and the one she, herself, would be, if she could: "Jesus, God, it is important to get to eighty." Leslie What speculates how life might be should she outlive her husband: "Three Sisters Have We in Our House." Lauren B. Davis portrays her new role as caregiver to a mom who is "breaking down." Laura McCullough presents a frank appraisal of what it's like to be ill within a dysfunctional healthcare system—"They broke my body down into parts." Hester L. Furey reflects on lives chiseled by indifferent and merciless nature. Carol Smallwood writes about her battle with cancer, describing how the ordinary has become extraordinary: ". . . the end of the coffee is best because sugar settles there." There is Clare MacQueen's heartbreaking portrayal of a mother's unimaginable loss, and Alicia Ostriker's admonition that "if you would only recognize that you are no more than that fly or that cloud / Everything would change, you would find yourself illuminated. . . ."

It's curious to note this *becoming*, the furrowed brows, the aches and pains, the troubles of bodies slowly declining in a world that grows ever more vibrant to each one of us because of the heightened awareness born of aging and the cherished bittersweet moments that enrich rather than diminish us. We don't look at all youthful anymore. But the images in our mirrors do not say it all, do they. They do not define us. It is the image in our minds that matter. And in our mind's eyes we are twenty-somethings, living life gifted with the knowledge and wisdom born of a more mature perspective, relieved of the heavy angst and narcissism of our teenage years. It is a perk of old age: the freedom to be who we are without mirrors, pretext, or apologies.

While aging involves no small amount of trepidation, the women contributors of *Winter Tales II* are no whiney sissies, choosing, instead, to explore the aging process through "a fragile dewdrop on its perilous way."

R.A. Rycraft
January 2012

Kelly Cherry

To Catullus—Highet

(A response to the Highet translation of Catullus 70)

My lover says he'd want to lie with none
But me, even if Venus herself welcomed his wooing.
Oh, yes! but what a man will say to an older woman,
write it on thin air, read on the run.

Gladys Swan

A Few Fragments

As age brings its various transitions, memory takes some interesting and problematic turns, not only with its various lapses and lacunae, but with what rises to the surface with differing responses and questions of meaning. Fragments from my childhood keep emerging, moments of intense emotion or memorable consequences, but now with a sense of distance. *Oh my—that happened sixty-odd years ago.* I recognize that these moments filled my mental horizon at the time, but in themselves they seem now but small markers on the path of becoming. And yet those incidents seem to have been sources of seminal experiences that have given shape to my life. They remain memorable even though they have now only the substance of dreams, partial and disembodied. They have appeared and gone like the house where I spent my childhood until I was ten, in Seaford, Delaware. When I went back to the town more than fifty years later, the whole neighborhood had ceased to exist, along with the antebellum house with the pillars in front and the porch swing that took me to Philadelphia, where I had never been—such a lovely set of sounds to which to put your breath.

The town had given up most of its moorings to the past and become something else. I was in a strange land. I could no longer find the train station with its water tower, where the train chuffed alongside. Nor the Sussex Hotel on the main street, nor the barbershop where I sat while my father got his hair cut—I loved the smell of witch hazel. Nor Mr. Longendyke's drug store with its year-round Christmas wreath, as though the whole notion of time had been let go entirely, jarring my sense of order. Nor the corner grocery, where Mr. Grogan reached up with his gripper for cereal boxes on the high shelves; nor the A&P, with its peculiar A&P smell—possibly manufactured somewhere?; nor the store with the pickle barrels and smelly cheeses across the street. Nor Bob Messick's little convenience store with its case of penny candy, jaw breakers and suckers, where I used to spend my penny or nickel on the way home from school—where I could take from the refrigerated case a chocolate-coated vanilla or an orange and vanilla popsicle. I can remember the taste of those popsicles, the coldness on the tongue, the taste of orange against the vanilla; the way the layer of chocolate broke and gave way to ice cream beneath. I can remember the satisfaction of eating one right down to the popsicle stick and the taste of wood. A hoard of little treasures.

These were certain pleasures, the way the sensation allowed a communication with what was out there, the way one was put in touch with it, came to know it, was carried along to other experiences of the senses. They were the small satisfactions that provided a foundation to an everyday reality. The feel of patent leather shoes, the thrill of climbing trees, the visual softness of twilight with a touch of coolness on the shoulders, the time of hide and seek and lightning bugs, and the great moth I once caught. I still remember the way it spiraled upward into the twilight sky when I released it. And I could sense something of its rise to freedom that, though I couldn't give a name to it, became, as I think about it, a point of reference.

Some form of the elementary school was still there, but not the field behind where I picked blackberries. In my imagination I can still feel the scratches on my legs from roaming among the vines, see the buckets of berries Margaret and Betty and I carried home. I recall the cherry tree in the vacant lot I climbed for the ripening cherries, the pies my mother made from them. Over the years I have picked wild strawberries, blueberries, raspberries, and blackberries in the Maine woods; peaches and plums from the trees in my yard, and I still feel the satisfaction of having that relationship with the fruits of the earth, the savors.

Within the classroom itself, I became acquainted with the delights of color. I still remember an image of a house among trees, done in lavenders and greens on the cover of one of my books, and thinking, Oh, if I could only paint a picture like that. I cherished the calendar pictures given to me by a printer my father knew when we visited his shop. These engendered some of my first aesthetic responses as I tried to draw pictures myself and model things in clay.

I can still see myself on the ground at recess playing marbles with the boys, still remember the ignominious defeat at the hands of a tall boy named Philip, with the loss of my favorite shooter. I was the only girl in my grade school of the marble-playing persuasion. I think marbles must also have been an early source of aesthetic pleasure, their colors, the feel of them in my hands, the way they shot out from the thumb. And the gaming quality they gave rise to. An early impulse to do the things boys did—I loved playing cars with the kids across the street, making roads among the tree roots, driving the abandoned cars at the back of the vacant lot, and climbing trees. Perhaps these activities carried a sense that there need be no necessary distinction between what boys and girls might do, a view that has stayed with me and which has unfolded with greater reality in the culture as time has passed.

The cemetery was the main thing in the town that had not disappeared, it being perhaps too heavy a set of objects to yield docilely to time. I remember the fear I had of walking through it on the way to school. And the extreme grief that rose from my first confrontation with death—when my cat died during the birth of her kittens. The rent her absence made in the fabric of things was beyond my comprehension, and my grief could not be assuaged. When I compare to it certain subsequent moments of emotional shock, I cannot say that they reached more deeply into the well of emotion or took my consciousness to any greater plane. Death had entered the world and marked a before and after. It brought a certain paradox. In itself that moment has left the sense only of a small incident: yes, cats do die; a number of cats have been part of my life. Yet it was an experience that shaped my life, reverberated through it, opened up a mystery that has never ceased to be. And I recognize from it that certain seminal experiences, seemingly insignificant in themselves, lift one's consciousness from its innocence or ignorance to a different plane, introducing motifs that spiral through one's life on different levels as the years go by. I can't even remember what the cat looked like.

No doubt many people are left with the vibrations of far more harrowing memories. Those who have experienced the horrors of torture and war and its savagery, the deaths of loved ones from natural disasters, earthquakes and tsunamis must find it hard to escape such nightmares, and no doubt relive those experiences again and again, long after their occurrence. But whatever their magnitude or consequences, each of us is left with her own sense of experience, what we have been shaped by, what has, in effect, created what we are. And yet all that creates us slips away.

I can't remember now when I became greatly preoccupied with the question of what experience actually is. Were there certain essential experiences you had to have in order to qualify as "having lived"? The question perhaps arose sometime in my early twenties when it seemed to me that nothing of consequence had ever happened to me, that my life had been so ordinary and boring, so without adventure that I must be totally deficient. I'd had no "experience." With a deep sense of deprivation, I felt something akin to despair. My husband had grown up in Los Angeles and had lived on North Beach in San Francisco, had been in the Navy during WWII on a destroyer escort in the South Pacific, and had been in the Korean War as well, had worked in potteries and in a hospital.

He had stories to tell. I had grown up in small towns in Delaware and New Mexico. I'd gone to school and read books.

As I went along, the question became more pressing and difficult to fathom. I met up with those whose lives held a good deal of incident and event, but who, on some level, didn't seem to have gained much except a few anecdotes or complaints, didn't seem to have had experience, whatever that meant. And the question became an underlying impulse to explore as a writer what I observed from other people and as I examined the events of my own life. Both from art and life I kept discovering that those episodes that cast a new light on things, that offered occasions for revelation, were not necessarily earthshaking: incidents of cruelty and kindness, betrayal and rescue, matters of obsession and denial, of anger and anguish, selfishness and generosity, courage and cowardice, joy and sorrow, or the circumstances that made known to us our predilections or values could be as insignificant as the cover of a third grade text book, the reality of the death of a cat as earthshaking and mysterious as any other death.

As I look back over the mounting decades, it appears to me that the movement toward consciousness is the great challenge of our lives, in its demand that we deal with our experience, confronting its mystery, its connection with suffering in the unfolding sense of what one is asked to do or be. In a curious way, I have come to both a sense of the mutability of all things and of something imperishable. At one point, a particularly painful episode in my life that I kept going over and over in my mind, the way the tongue keeps touching the hole from which a tooth has been pulled—the sense of betrayal was so strong, so wounding. I took long walks lost in my obsession. Then, quite suddenly, I knew that whatever had happened, including my emotions, would fall away like so much chaff and that something deeper, diamond-like, existed beneath it, that would remain untouched. And what was that? Something that went beyond immediate circumstances and personality, beyond the mask created for the world, and which allows us to play a part in it. Perhaps many parts. Something more real than any of the changing attributes of things, including the physical body we inhabit. Not that such moments of distress were at an end, nor the obsessive thinking they generated. But if I allowed myself, there was another point of reference, a sense that only the moment can be lived before it becomes a fading coal.

Now with so much of my life behind me, with so little of its material evidence left in the world, and the rest subject to the imperfections of memory, barely distinguishable from dream, it seems that my experience consists of those small, stunning parables of light that have marked my perceptions on the path of becoming: the deep impulse that sends one toward something of original authenticity—if Wordsworth's description of our birth as "but a sleep and a forgetting" is correct—before entering the final mystery.

Photo by Dan Miller

Elisabeth Murawski

voyage to the end

I sin so much harder now
knowing what I know

a sail snaps in the wind
I look the other way

a dream is returning
from the year

of my birth
to be transfigured

like a Da Vinci smile
a nightingale

parting the leaves
a melody

the silver-green
of corn husks

pouring a river
into the sea

redeeming
the Alamos I have lost

Leigh Anne Jasheway

The Theory of Aging Relativity

Even if you weren't good at physics in high school, chances are you understand the theory of aging relativity. This is the theory that states: "Relatively speaking, I won't be middle-aged until I'm dead." Which explains why at sixteen you thought thirty was ancient, but today thirty is *too young to make important decisions like voting and choosing a wardrobe.*

Einstein explained this phenomenon using the space/time continuum. He proved that it doesn't matter where you are in time, but how much *space* there is between your age and what you perceive as "old." And, the further you move along the timeline, the more space there must be. Thus, for many of us these days, "old" is not a term we use to refer to wine or moldy stuff in the back of the refrigerator, but rather to Neanderthal Man or the Great Pyramids.

Einstein also said that time slows as you approach a black hole. This is an important principle because many people feel that as they get older (or, relatively speaking, "closer to middle-aged"), time starts to fly by too quickly. Thus, the solution is obvious: hang out near a black hole—your doctor's waiting room, for example. You can see that Einstein was right, as time almost stands still while you're thumbing through a 1987 issue of *Highlights for Children*, trying to not be sneezed on by the patients on either side of you. The DMV is another black hole. A quick visit to renew your license and get a picture that looks more like a one-eyed troll with a hangover than you. The DMV not only slows things down, it can actually cause time to go in reverse.

Science can easily explain many of the things that happen as we get older. For example, there's the theory that for every action, there is an equal and opposite reaction. This is why, when your kids discover that you still have an active sex life, they react so violently. Just like you do when you hear the same about them. No one is to blame; it's just the scientific method.

Then there's the law of entropy, which states that: "Bodies in motion tend to stay in motion. Bodies at rest tend to stay at rest." Little known is the third part of this law which had been lost for years, but resurfaced recently as someone finally cleaned up the lab. The third part of the law states: "Bodies in movies and on TV tend to be figments of someone's imagination, so there's no reason to get worked up."

Last, but not least, there's the theory of matter and anti-matter. This theory holds that the more matter you accumulate as you age, the less it matters. Which is why a one-inch gain around your hips in your twenties is a crisis, while a six-inch gain in your fifties doesn't even make you break a sweat. After all, there are so many things that matter more than how you look in shorts.

Well, there you go. Everything you ever wanted to know about the physics of aging. Next month, maybe we'll explore logarithms! Or learn more about black holes.

Bette Lynch Husted

The View From Here

Strangely, it's the physical part that's easy—
sit-ups, pushups. I can still lift a backpack,
push the tips of cross-country skis through powder,
follow Coyote's

shadow into midsummer moonlight. Even
nursing homes don't frighten me like they used to.
Once my headlights caught a bent, hobbling woman
crossing the highway

in the rain: I cried out in horror. I was
younger then, a girl who could do Back Bridges—
arching like the St. Louis Gateway—but not
understand movement

when I saw it. Dancing across the kitchen
holding this old friend, this familiar body
in my arms (or in his: the same man who's loved me
more than three decades),

now I honor her. Yes, there's joint pain. Bone loss—
lace designs on X-rays. And though I swallow
Fosamax with faith born of desperation
(this Catechism

teaching antioxidants, chocolate, red wine),
something in me's already broken: Sam Stone
came home years ago, yet our cars are flying
flag decals as if

yellow-ribbon magnets will get us into
heaven this time. Bullets and greed, familiar
lies retold by all those familiar liars—
my generation

watching it come round again as though all those
dreams meant nothing . . . still, we awake each morning
pulled by something deeper than blood or bone, this
mystery that leads us

gently toward whatever awaits us. Older, I'll be
old soon. (Language hesitates, glancing backward.)
Carried with this tide, I'm a child still learning
how to breathe, swimming

through the curling wave of my mother's voice, earth-
power lifting me toward the stars, those heavens,
form becoming formlessness—*onward, outward,
nothing collapsing.*

Laurie Stone

Once you change the setting on an object, what does it become?

1

On the TV show *Mad Men*, Dick Whitman exchanges dog tags with his commanding officer, Don Draper, after the man is killed and disfigured in Korea. Dick doesn't think about the consequences. He can be here now. He swaps his life for Don's because he's tired of being Dick, with his hard-luck boyhood, and he imagines being Don will give him a leg up in the world. We admire the rash act. It's in our code. You want rashness, look at DNA—cells printing themselves like money, giving themselves away on the street saying, "Take me, hold me." When I met Richard, I chucked my New York life because even though it was home, I felt restless and unanchored. Richard was in a marriage he decided to leave, and so transplanted Brit united with New York Jew. Every promise invites a change of heart.

2

I am turning into the Chekhov play where the women stand at the window of their provincial outpost and pine for Moscow. Moscow, Moscow, Moscow is all you hear about in *The Three Sisters*. Moscow is society and surprise—all the things a great city is supposed to be.

In a city like that, the streets are your arteries and veins.

"You have the look of the last Tasmanian," Richard says, "the only speaker of your language." We're in Scottsdale, 2008. Before I moved here, he said: "You will miss your life, your friends." I said: "I can work anywhere." When has anything you thought about the future turned out right?

Technically, my apartment is still in my name, but seeing my friend Adam's belongings all around, I'm restless and unhappy. I have traveled before but never this far off course and not without knowing I was coming back. Can you hear me, Major Tom? We are all the only speakers of our language.

We visit Kierland Common, an outdoor shopping mall designed to look like a village with a square and a fountain in the center. The stores are the usual suspects: Barnes & Noble, Banana Republic, Eileen Fisher. Scattered about are a few pricey restaurants and a place you can get a sandwich, but this is not a neighborhood where people live. It's a shopping destination, and visitors arrive and depart by car. "It's based on Main Street, Disney," Richard says, "rather than an actual town square. It's an evocation of village centers that in reality have been abandoned." What a smarty-pants boyfriend I have. We're in Arizona because he teaches museum studies at the university, and he's in his element, the interpreter of spaces, and I'm glad. He's wearing a carrot-colored t-shirt, and his silvery hair spikes up. These streets are a break from the Valley's dominant suburban sprawl, punctuated by strip malls and condos, and I am trying to unstitch my old patterns. But who am I kidding? Kierland Common is depressing and not all that different from other sections of Scottsdale and Phoenix constructed by developers. There is no urban tangle to get lost in.

Richard asks why I am sighing, and I don't know I am, and the air between us gets a blue-black, funnel cloud look, and I say this place, this place where we live is an indistinct fuzzball, and in it I am a fuzzball, too, even though I have seedling friendships, people it takes an hour each way to see. I talk about the difference between an urban facsimile and a city that evolves as an emergent system, little bit by little bit, and is shaped by the language, clothes, art, and food of the people in its neighborhoods. Richard says all cities are constructed around commercial interests and that Western cities and Eastern cities are based on different models. He says what Eastern cities have is a patina of use and wear.

My head lights on fire and my voice grows emphatic, a pitch that sounds to him like yelling, and I say: "Are you suggesting that the difference between a mall and a city is soot?" And he says: "You like to fight, you just like to fight. You *need* to. It's something about you and your mother." And we are thinking, *Why did I abandon whatever the hell I had for this hidebound flame thrower.* But I am also thinking, *I would be just as lost in New York without my love.*

But my love is pissing me off with his crack about fighting, even though it's true. And why is he protecting Arizona? I say: "What's Arizona to you, huh? Every day when you write, you don't situate yourself here. You're in England, wandering down cobbled streets or trucking across windblown moors. Or you're in New York, listening to jazz or riding the subway and looking over your shoulder for muggers. You have hardly any friends here! So what's this defense of Arizona?" And he says: "There's something to what you say, but I feel that badmouthing Arizona is snobbish and an easy target for outsiders. I just hate snobbery." And I say: "Well, I'm not a snob, and I want to talk about my experience without being accused of attacking people." And he shoots me a grumpy smile, and I see his even row of top teeth. It hurts him if I'm unhappy in the place he has brought me to. How can I forget it hurts him? He says: "What the hell am I defending?" And it hits us we're defending ourselves against being swallowed up in the other, and I think I could talk to this man for the rest of my life. I mean, really, how much longer do I have?

3

I sleep close to Richard, because he bunches the covers to his side. Last night he said he was too tired to pack. He said, "Why do we have to go to New York? Why don't you go without me?" At the thought of being there alone, the little rubber stopper that holds in my happiness falls out. I picture us walking, my arm around his waist. When I actually do this, he says, "I can't walk that way." He slings his arm around my back and pulls me toward him like a Siamese twin. "Can you walk this way?"

In the morning, when I see him at the table, his diabetic supplies are in a jumble, and I say, "This always happens before a trip." He says, "It does?" Today, defective tubing is at fault, but now Richard won't have time to iron his shirts and pack carefully. I look in the mirror and say, "I am going on the plane with bed hair and puffy eyes."

He needs breakfast. I water the plants. He showers. I take out the garbage and mail the envelope to Netflix. Domestic life. Why does it feel like so much work? I throw a few belongings on the floor near our bag. He stares. I say, "What? I'm going to fold them." He says, "Yes, but, oh well, never mind, I have a system, and, well, never mind, it's fine, you always pack like that."

I am wearing my black pants and black jersey and bed hair, and it's time to toast bread for sandwiches. Richard's hair looks fluffy, and he's unconcerned about food. He thinks we won't get seats on the earlier flight we're trying to catch and will wind up marooned at the airport for eight hours. He says, "Why are we going stand-by? Why do you have to squeeze every possible minute into New York, eh, what's your problem, Phoenix isn't good enough for you, this place where I have exiled myself for God knows how many years isn't interesting enough for you?" I say, "Yes, darling, that's right."

Bill, who will drive us to the airport so we can leave our car at his house, is standing outside when we pull up. He's wearing one of those silk shirts he bought after Richard started wearing them.

He's been having a tough time at work, having run down his job so effectively he's been left behind. He wearies Richard, but he's also Richard's best friend, and as I see his yearning eyes and handsome face, my heart warms right up, and I think this must happen to Richard when he and Bill struggle. This must be the way Richard takes me back, too. I look at the swerve of Richard's arrow body, and I think, mine, whoever you are.

In a café on 8ᵗʰ Street, I notice a woman with high cheekbones and a smudge of charcoal hair. She looks familiar. She looks like me. As Richard and I climb the stairs to my friend Lee's apartment, we see her talking to the doorman below, and I realize she's Emily, come with her photographer friend to shoot my picture for an anthology she is editing. We have only talked on the phone, but we embrace. She wears a cape over a sweater and floppy pants—soft and elegant. She says I look happy. I'm in the city with Richard. I look happy.

Richard and I are on the subway when he has this thought: Maybe I got together with Laurie so I could return to New York. During his first ten years in the States, he and Suzanne lived on the Upper West Side and in Park Slope. He keeps the subway thought to himself for a few days, then over tea this morning discloses it like a toad he's pocketed.

"Why didn't you tell me before?"

He looks at his cup. "I thought you might feel instrumental."

"Make me an instrument! As long as we get back here!" I touch the top of his hand. "Of course you had to think about what I could do for you, what you were trading your life for." And I see his soft smile and shrewd eyes. I see him thinking: *You had better be able to hold two opposing thoughts in your mind at the same time.*

I am musing on this conversation as Emily's photographer snaps my picture. I smile. Several times the photographer and Emily ask me not to smile, but my mouth looks funny if I don't. It looks like something bad has happened to my face. After the shoot, we eat fruitcake and the pair leaves.

Then Richard reads me a story by Lydia Davis, in which a divorced woman recalls a time in Paris when a fish bone gets caught in her ex-husband's throat. Attempts to dislodge it with bread and water fail, and the man's throat becomes inflamed. They move onto the streets in search of aid, and strangers direct them to a hospital where a skilled young doctor extracts the bone with a tiny hook. The narrator remembers that the doctor is Jewish and that her ex-husband, also a Jew, speaks in French to the doctor about being Jews. The story is suspenseful: will he or won't he be relieved of the bone? But I have no idea what it's about.

"Connection," Richard says. "The bone links the ex-couple to each other, propels them into the world, and forms a happy memory of their life together. The story is about the risk the narrator takes by recalling happiness during a time of separation." Before reading to me, he said Emily may really have liked me but I frustrated her wish to capture a serious expression. "Her book is about loss and aging, for god's sake, and there you were looking like a cat lapping cream." I think about how much better Richard is at understanding people than I am, but now he's erased my happy memory of Emily.

We are waiting for Adam. An hour before he was supposed to have arrived, he called to ask if he could carry on reading Heidegger for another half hour. I said sure but I was thinking, *Carry on reading Heidegger! You god damn read Heidegger every day of your life! Richard and I are hardly ever in New York!* I was thinking what's the point of being in a place where I have friends when my friends are jerks? In Arizona, at least I can pretend otherwise.

When Adam shows up, he's grim-faced and nervous as a squirrel who can't remember where he stored his nuts. He squirms on his chair and loses the thread of his conversation. He has a problem with his mother. He has a problem with his ex-wife. He has a problem with his daughter. He has no problem with Heidegger. The German philosopher does not come up.

After he leaves, I say to Richard, "He thinks I'm not smart

enough to share his work with."

"No, talking about ideas is his version of intimacy with you, and he won't do it unless you can be alone."

I don't think this is true, but I keep it to myself because I am trimming the Talmudic, "Yes, maybe, but" rejoinders that wear Richard out. He comes from people who say, "That's right, of course" while thinking, "You gigantic idiot." In Richard's family, you act like it's the Blitz every day and displeasure is rude and unpatriotic. You can't even return something to a store, lest you arouse the hatred of the clerks who don't want to be reminded they are there to provide service. This stuff puts my teeth on edge, but what are you going to do?

Richard wants to be alone with me, so he imagines other people do, too. I think Adam can't be bothered to make connection. There's a bone in his throat that will never be lifted out.

A few days later I speak to him, and he says he felt shoehorned into our schedule and thought we didn't care about him. He had invited Richard to the Guggenheim Museum, and Richard had ducked out. My sweetheart was the one Adam had wanted to be alone with.

I tell this to Richard, and he says, "Irritation is at the center of everyone's story, irritation that can neither be coughed up or swallowed. That's what Lydia Davis was writing about."

I think if Richard is this smart, I should ignore whatever else is wrong with him. Then I consider things you could object to. When Suzanne was angry, she sent him a long list. No one could fault her. She was startled to realize that her old shoe could be someone else's prize, even though this is the principle behind thrift shops.

Suzanne disliked attending "the sick bed," as she called it. That goes with the territory of a type 1 diabetic. It means you sometimes wake up and begin a conversation, and it takes a while to notice Richard is saying, "Open the birds," or "I forgot my elbow." He's sweating. When you tell him he's having a low sugar, he denies it angrily. Belligerence is one of the symptoms of the condition, but this form of anger looks just like his regular anger, so you have to grab one of his fingers and press a little spring-loaded device against it and squeeze out a drop of blood onto a testing strip in the glaucometer. After that you make him eat glucose tablets and toast with jam. Sometimes, in a low sugar, he forgets who he is and loses language all together, and in high sugars he becomes sluggish and sick to his stomach. All this makes me tender.

Suzanne frowned on the amount of space Richard takes up at dinner parties with opinions and anecdotes. She thought he should listen more, while I encourage him because usually he's drowning out someone else who is boring.

When I consider the ways we are compatible and the charming curve of Richard's ass, I am happy to have no exit strategy, although sometimes I think this is asking for trouble and I should pack a bag just in case.

Bette Lynch Husted

being women, being sixty

who knew
it would be
about love
at sixty

there he goes
with it now
every poem
every vow

here he comes
rose in vase
excuses
in place

we are wind
softened stones
we are girls
we are crones

dancing still
in these bones
no one owns

Jan Eliot

No Little Old Ladies Allowed

Renée Ashley

Eighty

I am eighty, surely I am
eighty, though my ticket to birth
states unequivocally thirty-seven, thirty
and seven, the year forty-nine, and still
I am eighty, surely, born like any other
fat white baby, born like the juicy, irresponsible
pale and blue-eyed flesh I still am. Jesus,
God, it is important to get to eighty.

In order to be eighty, one must be
wise, I am told, wise, as they say, as
the sages. It is not true. I am eighty,
eighty in the marrow, eighty in that crucial
spot behind the eyes, eighty, eighty is old, but not
old. Eighty is too damn smart for one's own
salvation, too damn late, too compact, too much vital
information stored in the creases. Well
then, eighty is not what I am. Eighty
is what I would be, if I could.

My mother is nearly eighty, then. My mother
who is the mainstay, the corset stay, the bone,
the ecru and folded, cut-on-the-bias silk night

dress, that mother is nearly eighty—she, round
as an apple, taller than I by one mere inch
or two and, don't you forget it, damn
proud of it. Some joke that. Some joke,
my mother at nearly eighty, slower, yes,
but kinder, fat as butter, and right
as only near-eighty can be, right hind-
sight, right miraculous, backwards and forwards
right, comprehension, applied, served with understanding and enough recognition to keep it to one's
self. Eighty.

Ursula K. Le Guin

The Long Becoming

It takes so long to learn to be a woman.
Body's got hormones on its side, but mind
needs years and years to work at being human,

at how to understand the long becoming,
and what there is to lose and what to find,
and ways it might be good to be a woman,

honest, and compassionate, and common,
to be impartial as the summer wind,
to use the years as paths toward being human.

Men aren't much use so long as they keep claiming
to lead the way and rule the holy land
and own what they ignore, the ways of women.

It's up to us to own ourselves, and by naming
ourselves declare what we have always owned,
our right to say what it is to be human.

The years betray us, though. They keep consuming
body and mind and all we've thought and found.
It takes too long to learn to be a woman,
our time runs out before we're halfway human.

Ursula K. Le Guin

The Arts of Old Age

I learn the arts of old age day by day,
the expertise of being lame; the sense
of unimpatient impotence;
the irony of all accomplishments;
the silent, furtive welcome of delay.

Roisin McLean

White Chin Hair & a Lonely Female Cardinal

You wake in a start. The clock's red LED numbers on the top shelf of the light-hued Scandinavian computer hutch in the corner say 8:32, and you're surprised the morning birdsong hasn't awakened you sooner. Not really—you sleep later and later these days. You peek out the shade. No car in the driveway. Your daughter must have left early for church. Nature calls immediately, as it always does now, and the TV and high, neatly-arranged DVD stacks on the bureau obscure the reflection in the mirror of everything below your nude upper torso as you rush past and bounce only once off the doorframe—*once* being a nice change.

During ablutions, while you critically assess your physical self in the mirror above the sink, you recall the titillating words of a sweet silver-haired man who looked up at you mid-"dalliance" a week or month ago. "You have the breasts of a teenager," he said with glee, his face aglow. Which now makes you toss your once-brunette, then-white, now-platinum-blonde mane in a happy perky shy way that ill suits your new age of sixty but not your current state of mind. Your divorce from that expletive-deleted deserter will be final soon, and it seems important to take stock of things anew. One thing at a time, you've learned, one compartmentalized area of your brain at a time—otherwise, the whole picture looms panoramic as a tidal wave. The bathroom mirror doesn't reveal the whole picture of your body, however. Since this seems to be the day you will take stock of your physicality—and why not, church doesn't do it for you anymore, and your unemployed days for months have been spent in little more than stupor—you sashay naked down the hall to your daughter's room and the full-length mirror on her closet door.

The light is brighter here. The crooked scar radiating out from your right nipple, where a suspicious mass one-quarter the size of your breast was excised from the inside, is fading with time. (You don't remember the pain.) Post-biopsy, the mass proved to consist of not one but five pre-cancerous tissues. For two years post-surgery, the nipple remained numb, which creeped you out sufficiently that you simply stopped touching it, and your husband, still around then, had long before lost interest in your nipples—and your mind, for that matter.

At least the surgeon sewed you back up so that it still looks like a breast. Most of the women on both sides of your family had their breasts lopped off during their fifties but too late to save their lives. Grateful to still have your right breast, you cup it and touch the nipple, feel the nipple feel the touch, watch the nipple perk up hard, feel the pleasant sensation lower down. Which makes you laugh—you'd assumed since youth, even though no one ever told you, that sexual desire just stopped, like growth of wisdom teeth and menstruation. Seriously, what mother would speak of such a thing? Would you tell your daughter? Maybe. When she's forty or fifty. Whenever she realizes life is not a never-ending promise.

A promise of what, you wonder. That seems an issue for another day, and you glance at your inner arms and sigh. You've been heaving those eight-pound dumbbells backward over each shoulder for months now, and you've still got wrinkly jello to show for your dedication. Despite the forty pounds you lost, sick with betrayal and hypomania, after your husband left. You don't want to marry again, so what difference does it make what shape your body is in, you wonder. Tons, you answer. *You* care, you're right to care, and that's what counts—taking good care of yourself, jello and all.

Your eyes scan lower, down to the waist that was always too wide. A twelve-inch difference between bust size and waist and between hip size and waist? Only a man could have determined those dimensions, which you tried futilely to fulfill for far too long. Was any female ever 36-24-36? Maybe Marilyn Monroe, but look what it got her. Or Barbie. No, actually she's about 5-3-5 and if proportionally human size would lack the requisite body fat to menstruate. So you're stuck with 39-33-37, which isn't really *that* displeasing, you decide. Except when you look at that wrinkled pouch (as wide as your hip circumference, and why can't the proverbial "they" cut clothing for this particular problem) that juts out above the six-inch-wide Caesarian section scar, where another surgeon's knife bisected a muscle, which cannot ever resume normal function. But, you conclude, the scar performs a most beneficial function; it mirrors the smile on your face every time you think of your daughter, and what greater joy is there than that.

Moving on, your eyes settle on the saddle bags, which for whatever reason you never worried about. Down to the knobby knees. The right knee bulges more than the left, permanently swollen, where yet another surgeon's knife performed an arthroscopy when you were fifty to trim both torn lateral and medial menisci and remove the shredded ACL. A surgery usually performed on professional football players who are bashed, thrown, and then buried below a massive heap of Hulk-size men. All you did was step on your dog's leash, as the obedience trainer instructed, your dog bolted, the bottom half of your leg went one way and the upper half the other, and the next thing you perceived was gravel from the parking lot poking into your back. No matter that you couldn't walk for three weeks or that the recovery period lasted fourteen months, not three. Water under the bridge. You've mastered the exercises that keep your quads strong enough to compensate for that mysterious ACL, which looks like a thin stick of gum but is deceptive, has incredible tensile strength, weaves through the knee and maintains its stability under normal, but not all, circumstances. You bow and give quads their due.

Your calves, nicely curved and muscled, pass muster. Your feet are too tiny for your height, which is why you're a klutz and can stumble on a wisp of dandelion fuzz, but men seem to like tiny feet. Especially with toenail polish. Why should it matter, your feminist self demands. Because you care, you answer. Because you want a man again. As absurd as that may seem at age sixty. Or maybe it's not absurd. No one ever told you about that either.

So your body "is what it is"—damn the cliché—and can only get worse, not better. Yet that's OK, you decide with maturity. Which is when you gasp and spin terrified to face your daughter's bed. No one is there. Not like a few Sundays ago when you thought you had the house to yourself, so didn't bother to shut your bedroom door when you catered to your personal "whims," indulging in sighs and moans fit for a celebratory queen, only to discover with horror once your daughter returned from church that her boyfriend was lying upstairs in her bed the whole time—and wide awake, he made a point of telling you later, but with no telltale smirk or horror of his own. Not the sort of embarrassment you ever expect at age sixty. Falling and breaking a hip, sprouting a dowager's hump, yes, but not … you can't even give this unspeakable thing a name. You shudder. Hardly auspicious for the decade to come. Your shoulders hunch.

Car tires crunch gravel in the driveway. You race into your room to dress. Black jeans, a V-neck teal sweater. You take the stairs quickly, hand gripping the rail tightly—second nature for ten years now since the knee fiasco—anxious to bask in the joy on your daughter's face after she teaches Sunday school. Where is she? You open the back door, which she forgot to lock on her way out, again. No car in the driveway. You hear the faint strains of "Neverland"— your hearing's still keen—and race back up the stairs for your cell phone in your pocketbook, tucked under the bed in case of burglary (like burglars would fail to look there).

"Hey, Mum," your daughter greets you. "I forgot to stop at Panera. My treat. Do you want anything?"

"Are you driving while you're talking on the cell phone?" you ask.

"I'm at the red light at Eagle Rock and Mt. Pleasant." Her undisguised disgust lowers the pitch of her voice.

"Sorry, sweetie. It's that 'ole Mom thing.' I'd love a lemon poppy seed muffin and a large dark roast coffee. Thanks."

"No prob, Mum," she says, so she's already forgiven you, but she's off the wireless line before you can say "I love you."

You wander back downstairs to the kitchen where you nuke a cup of Irish Breakfast tea before you realize how dumb a move that is, coffee and all on its way. On the sofa in the living room while you're sipping your tea—which you'll throw down the drain as soon as you hear tires on the driveway again in order to avoid the embarrassment of explaining how quickly you forgot blah-blah-blah—you hear a strange sound in the kitchen. Probably just the Rose of Sharon branches brushing the windows. But it repeats. *Flap-tap-whoosh*. Again. And again.

Your steps across the Berber carpet are silent, and you tiptoe barefoot along the vinyl flooring past the basement door to peer around the stove. A female cardinal perches in the Rose of Sharon. She flings herself full force into the window, *flap-tap*, falls in a *whoosh* to the outer ledge, and peeks up and inside to the little ceramic statue of three open-mouthed hungry chicks, not cardinals, on the inner ledge. She retreats to the Rose of Sharon and repeats her dangerous, flinging *flap-tap-whoosh*.

You can't bear the thought of her breaking her neck. Before you can rap lightly on the window, she's gone in a flash of rustling leaves. A pair of cardinals, which mate for life, adopted your backyard years ago, and the joy of their presence dissolved over time into something you took for granted. You recall seeing the male, a handsome scarlet fellow, last Spring. It can't be empty-nest syndrome crazing the female; it's October. Has a neighborhood cat got her mate? Has he died of old age? You wish you could help this suffering female before she commits suicide.

"Neverland" plays again.

"I'm stopping at Shoprite, too," your daughter says. "We're out of milk. Want some fresh salmon for dinner?"

You try to explain in a somewhat hysterical confused rush about the female cardinal, but your daughter's in a rush, too. "Mum, what do you want?"

You agree to salmon and find yourself standing at the kitchen window weeping. "What *do* you want?" you ask yourself. The tears run to your chin before you wipe them with your hand and feel the stubble of one thick, strong, stubborn fiber, which you somehow missed during the neck- and chin-shaving ritual that—so help you, you can't think of in any way other than masculine—is now part of your daily *feminine* ablutions. At the downstairs bathroom mirror, it seems the stubble is invisible. Well, not quite, you discover. It's still a miracle, though. Your chin hair is finally turning white—you won't have to shave anymore! At which you suspect you've wasted the morning on shame-on-you shallow ruminations.

Back at the kitchen window, you bend that stubborn sole stubble this way and that with your index finger as you ponder again what you want out of life between now and the promise of life's end. In your mind's eye, you see reflected in the kitchen window the flame of a lone candle. It is night, and the soft shush of snow outside turns the landscape pointillistic, coats the ground with a warm, downy quilt, heaps high atop the bird-feeder for the lonely female cardinal (you feel her pain). In the window's reflection, you see yourself alone (you feel your pain). Then a man with a white beard joins you, hands you a glass cup of eggnog laced with rum. He rubs his beard against your cheek, your chin. You rub back and smile, secure in the knowledge that he can't feel your white stubble against his, that he knows you have white stubble, that he doesn't care a whit about it. As the peace outside and in envelops you, you feel his arm circle your not-24-inch waist, and you respond in kind. That *simple*, you think. It's hardly a young girl's dream. Is it the dream of the inner child in your sixty-year-old body? Maybe so. A winter-tale dream for comfort, or an "After" photo if you wish for more than dreams.

The driveway gravel crunches. You wake from your winter tale, wish for more than dreams, and smell the coffee, rich, mellow, and round.

Michelle Bitting

Patti Smith—after the premiere of "Dream of Life"

On the street outside The Aero Theatre,
two women puzzle
under the late summer stars,
dumbstruck in their L'Oréal lips
and pastel sweaters
by the unconventional allure
of the Godmother of Punk.
Where is the beauty?
they are wondering,
about her mannish mug,
the razor chin and dingy teeth,
her unshaved pits,
the way she stomps around the stage
in heavy black boots,
her faded peace sign t-shirt
drenched with rock star sweat.
What is it about her,
blindfolded, arms raised,
clapping to the hellfire
heavens as the audience belts
the soaring refrain:
G—l—o—r—i—a . . . Gloooooria!

like some ecstatic shaman,
whiskers of white spittle
sprouting down her chin.
She's spewing Rimbaud,
Ginsberg, Baudelaire,
a long silver cross
slung across her chest,
as the airborne audience
howls and stamps its collective feet,
the wings of her scraggly hair
flapping open and shut
around her urgent, transfixed face.
Singer or saint? Like me,
these ladies want to know,
as they fumble for their keys,
yakking away as cars buzz past
and the red marquee fizzles out.
They want to know
but there are no answers,
only the rush
of being baptized
for two cinematic hours
in the golden showers
of a factory girl from Jersey
who moved to New York City,
opened her cowboy mouth cave
and felt it ripen,
burst like a grape
in the cosmopolitan sun.
Don't you wish you wrote
those wild, edgy songs,
trashed the Chelsea Hotel
with Sam Shepard,

CBGB's and going platinum
only to take the money
and run to raise two kids
in the suburbs of Detroit?
In your fifties you re-emerge,
reinvent yourself,
rock 'n rolling the world stage
from Seattle to Berlin.
And when you're not
chanting for crowds,
inhaling a microphone
or fondling the pebbly contents
of an ancient Persian urn
filled with Mapplethorpe's ashes,
or being interviewed
for some bitchin' documentary,
ten years in the making,
you are tracking Blake's ghost
through the cemeteries, parks,
and urinals of Paris,
every place his bony,
misunderstood ass
is known to have squatted
and scribbled something beautiful
while taking an ordinary,
everyday, entirely human piss.

Hester L. Furey

Grief Tooth

What cracked you, number 18?
Money? Rage? Writer's block?
Six years of uncollected child support,
the student loan that will surely outlive me,
the academic career that didn't happen?
The marvelous children who have grown up,
little fish who swam away from the spring
into that broad, warm, murky river
where I can't protect them anymore?
Or the one sleeping warm and oblivious
at my side?

What finally caused you to give?
I know it wasn't really the hemp flakes.
Was it the weight of my unfinished work,
my dread at facing again
that backwards mineshaft where
I labor in the darkness to be born again?
Rage at my long-dead easy-living parents,
or lingering grief at their loss?
Was it all the injustice I swallowed,
because I could do nothing for it?
My war-mad country, gone off the track?
On the altar there's a stack of problems

I supposedly gave to God,
but I lied.

Not strong enough to let them go,
my right hand aches even in sleep.
I lie here and listen to the storm
boom its way eastward, from
a city insufficiently burned,
over to my blooming yard in Decatur.
Even in darkness its colors glow.
Only there can I accept mercy.
I don't want to join
Amis, Nabokov, Joyce, or
nameless legions of
Freud's impotent dreamers.
Let someone else mill this grain,
find the right word, make things nice.
Tonight I want only to sleep:
to drop like a stone and wake sharp,
fangs intact.

Supriya Bhatnagar

Memories and Misgivings

Yesterday, when I called Anju's house, I let the phone ring while making *chapattis* for dinner. The answering machine with her voice on it was a jolt. I had meant to hang up after a few rings if her husband did not pick up, and I *had not* wanted the machine to come on. After a seven-month battle with cancer, Anju, my friend of almost thirty years, died on a crisp March day. She was two months short of her forty-ninth birthday. The disease had ravaged her body and destroyed her organs. She described the pain as someone scooping out her insides with a knife and then rubbing chili pepper in the wound. In the end, we just waited for her to go.

Death had visited me earlier, but that was a long time ago, when my father died just before my tenth birthday. And then we got on with our lives—my mother, sister, and I—putting Death aside. I had to grow up first, write, study, write some more, meet my soulmate, marry, continue to write, have children, watch them grow as I struggled to write, and then be there as my children did all that I did. That was an unexpected death—Daddy dying at thirty-nine—and now, even with my turning fifty, Death is a distant cousin, one that I do not think of at all. Anju's dying, however, brought Death back to us.

Anju painted. I wrote, and she did oil colors. I used words to express my feelings. She could translate her thoughts into color and brush strokes—she would explain the meaning of each canvas as I admired her work. Our aging process showed in her strokes as her paintings took on a more metaphorical and philosophical stance.

We used words to express that stance, but visually they were there on the canvas, translated into shapes and swirls and colors.

Long before we vetted the philosophy of life and discussed the impact of religion, Anju and I knitted tiny woolen booties and sweaters and caps when we were pregnant together—each on our second pregnancy. She helped me with mine as I was expecting twins, and she had already finished hers for her baby. Our talks and discussions never contemplated the fact that either one of us could be gone before the children in our tummies reached adulthood.

§

Hindu philosophy divides our lives into Ashramas. An *Ashrama* (*āśrama*) in Hinduism is one of four stages in an age-based social system as laid out in the *Manu Smrti* and later Classical Sanskrit texts. Each stage of the human life has twenty-five years in it, based upon the assumption that one will live for a hundred years. Anju and I had finished the *Brahmacharya*—student life, and were now in the *Grihastha*—the household life. Soon we would have entered the *Vanaprastha*—the retired life. And we never even considered going through the *Sanyasa*—the renounced life.

The retired life would give us the maturity we needed—to give a deeper meaning to her paintings and to give authority to my writing. After all, we had the experience to know what we were expressing. Age granted us that authority. It gave us that cloak of respectability—our thoughts and words and canvases could have a deeper meaning.

§

When it comes to writing, I am a procrastinator. There is always a tomorrow or a new month or the next year. But is there, really? In school, we memorized Kabir's *Dohas* (couplets). Their rhyme and alliteration delighted the tongue. They were the nursery rhymes of our teenage years, and we never paused to give thought to what they actually meant. The famous 14th-century Indian poet expressed the most profound thoughts in the simplest of words:

Kaal Kare So Aaj Kar, Aaj Kare So Ub
Pal Mein Pralaya Hoyegi, Bahuri Karoge Kub
[Tomorrow's work do today, today's work now
if the moment is lost, the work be done how]

§

Now, I find it hard to concentrate on my writing knowing that Anju does not have that tomorrow. Or the next month. Or the next year. She left her last canvas unfinished. Just like her life.

I am also a closet hypochondriac. If my body itches, I am reminded of how Anju's liver malfunctioned. Will my dark skin show the jaundice that made hers turn yellow? If I have stomach cramps, I am reminded of my removed gallbladder and the consequences of it not being inside me. If my chest hurts, I am reminded of the heart attack that killed Daddy instantly. I feel my heart fluttering rapidly sometimes, but at other times it is the pain in my breasts, or a twinge in my uterus. And what about my ovaries? The silent cancer. I remember seeing Gene Wilder's stricken face on TV after Gilda Radner died of that disease. One of my uncles died of throat cancer, and cancer ate away at another uncle's kidneys until it killed him. How many body parts am I to worry about? I stand naked in front of the bathroom mirror, trying to see if there is puckering around the nipples on my breasts. I feel them regularly, but will I actually know what a lump is? Or is it just a fibroid that moves under my probing fingers?

§

In spirit, I do not feel any differently at fifty than I did after turning

58

forty. But to quantify that time can be depressing—ten years of lost opportunities, ten years' worth of more traveling I could have done, ten years' worth of words I could have put down on paper, ten years of more time I could have spent with my friend ...

"I would have liked to see more of the world, Supriya," Anju said one day while I sat with her during her illness. "You will, Anju, you will ..." Empty words ... empty promises ...

I flip through old photographs sometimes, when I have the time—time spent with family and friends—just to remind myself of what was. My three boys as babies, their friends, all grown now just like them. I see Anju's boys too, along with mine.

"It is exciting to know they will have girlfriends soon," she had said once. Simple things, simple pleasures that we had looked forward to.

Guilt is a heavy word ... a heavy feeling. I am alive ... she is not.

"These are the consequences of the misdeeds of a past life," she said about her illness. I had no response to that. Did I believe in past and future lives? Was this her *Karma* then?

Karma in Hinduism broadly names the universal principle of cause and effect and action and reaction that governs our lives. *Karma* is not a punishment, but rather a consequence of natural acts. It is a person's fate. I would rather have the misdeeds of the present life affect the current life and not wait for a rebirth. Anju then would have paid for her misdeeds earlier on.

"I need *moksha,* Suppy," my dear uncle, ill and in the last stages of cancer that started in his kidneys, had said to me when I went to visit him. The Sanskrit word *moksha* is a release from the cycle of birth and death. The body is the only thing that dies, but the soul lives on and is not subjected to occupying a body again and again. Daddy's death was a sudden occurrence. We could not hold on. But my uncle then ... and Anju now ... before we got used to the fact that she was sick, she was gone. It was hard to let go. I don't care if the soul lives on; I want the body with it.

§

I try to eat right and exercise regularly. And I tell myself that I do all that for my health and not to only "look good." "Thin" is everywhere—Bollywood heroines are thin, top fashion models are thin. But "thin" is something I never was. I do look thinner now at fifty than I did ten years ago, and am proud of that. But is that enough? The joints in my body do not care how thin I am. They only know how old I am and so have started acting up.

"No! No!" I tell the aches and pains. "Can't you see? You are not supposed to be here yet," but to no avail. The pain is here to stay.

Anju exercised regularly and ate right also. She did that better than I and that makes me angry. Why could not her body have rewarded her for that? Why attack her and kill her?

Inevitability is what makes me tolerate my many aches and pains. If my entering the next decade of my life means living with these minor irritabilities, so be it. Tolerance is an important Hindu virtue along with *Ahimsa* (nonviolence)—which is easy to follow; hospitality; compassion; respect; morality; austerity—which is difficult; wisdom; honesty; cleanliness; and celibacy—which is impossible. And so, I will tolerate the fact that I am getting older.

Mummy was a grandmother by the time she turned fifty and my grandmother was one many times over by the time she had her fiftieth birthday. Perceptions change. My grandmother looked older at fifty than my mother did, but I do not use words that convey "old" for myself. My boys have yet to find girls for themselves, and the term "grandmother" is something I have not thought about much.

Daddy is a distant memory now, and I have to pause to remember my dear uncles. Soon, I am afraid, we will get used to the fact that Anju will never come back. I will, however, continue to wonder about the "what ifs" and "what nots" had she not fallen ill and died. I will continue to write, penning thoughts on paper, and I will, as we all shall, go on with life, which has a strange way of thrusting us forward, regardless.

Laura McCullough

w/hole

Part I: Systems Thinking

—the process of understanding how the parts
within a whole work, such as ecosystems,
but also between people and in organizations.

They broke my body down into parts: 85% chance
        colon; 75% uterine; 12% ovarian; 50% ureter;
oh, there were numbers for the ileum, stomach,
        pancreas, and the brain. All I'd left, it seemed,
were my breasts which weren't endangered. So
        I wore a push-up to the meeting with the surgeon,
and she was nice, commented on my hand-crafted,
        silk shirt, and then said, Yes, *we* do *have to do*
a rectal, so I can check your ovaries from behind,
        and I said, well, nothing at all, but looked up
at the picture of a deep blue ocean with palm
        trees taped to the acoustic tile above me,
someone had placed there in a moment of empathy,
        because most of us, women at least, have lain
this way, with the heels of our feet in the metal
        cups—stirrups, not quite accurate, implying
we're the riders, when we're not; rather, we

are supine, surrendering to this exam or that,
today for the uterus, how it has to come out,
            and the ovaries, *castration*, not the word
used for females, but accurate. Later, it will be
            the other systems, piece by piece, til I have a bag
on one hip for one system, then on the other,
            and yes, I will go on, to *lead a full life*. First,
the reproductive system though. *You're done*
            with that, right? Besides, she says, *You both*
have jobs and kids; when do you have time
            for sex anyway? My step mother died this year
at 61. Lung cancer, then the brain. In the end,
            she was emaciated, except for her breasts,
implants she'd gotten at fifty, wanting, finally,
            to look the way she'd always desired. It was
all that was left of her, really, those perky
            bags under the white lace nightgowns. But,
she'd chosen them, you know, so they were part
            of her, how she saw herself. I get off the table
and clean myself. *You won't lose the vagina*, she
            tells me; *you can still have penetration.* I think
how she will penetrate me, grind up the meat
            of my insides and pull them through that hole,
how convenient. I think of how that is *one*
            system down. I think of a hole in the ceiling
behind the ripped off Caribbean calendar photo
            or a rust spot or a leak stain, how things
are covered up when they can't be fixed,
            how my step mom was carried out in
a plastic bag, bones and useless flesh, how the valet
            takes my ticket and brings me my car,
and smiles when I tip him, so I click my high heels,
            then sit into the car and lift my legs inside

and smooth my shirt down over my breasts,
　　　　　and turn the key to start my engine.

Part II: How To Kill Nutgrass

—the best way to kill nutgrass is with chemical
herbicides since it is so hard to get all the root out,
but this has safety and environmental consequences.

And I enter the hole of the tunnel ahead of me—
the Turnpike, Route 287, the Garden State Parkway—
time stopping where they come into confluence,　　　and,

nearing home,　there,　　　　　on the side of the road,
after the flood, is my neighbor, Mart, 67,
his wife, 61, with metastatic brain cancer;

they drilled a hole in her skull for the chemo,
just like Stephen whom they also drilled into,
the bone burning away,　　　　the matter exposed,

the room going dark as he receded into the aphotic tunnel
when they stimmed the wrong spot,　　　　and she, Jeanne,
with the cancer in her mind, can no longer write her name;

she is nameless on paper, but in the room inside her
where she somehow continues to live, she is a ghost of herself
trying to remember herself,　　　　which is why Mart

is on the side of the road which is his lawn,
sitting cross-legged like a boy yanking at the nutgrass
with one hand, the other poking the dirt with a spade,

a trail of holes behind him where he's succeeded,
a pile of the crab-like grasses with their exposed roots to his side,
and a smile on his face because he is getting his lawn back,

and the sun is shining, and he is alone for a few minutes
with his rump in the moist earth;   and Stephen is driving
across the surface of the world toward his next poems,

and I am driving now out of the tunnel of my unconscious
off all those roads it takes to go from one place to the next,
into my own driveway,   black asphalt,   the image

of palm trees covering a water stain like an afterimage on my retina,
the sun another afterimage if I look hard and then squeeze shut my face.
Mart is waving now,   waving as I step out of the car,

his pain meter low today,   mine on hold,   Stephen's brain
pace-maker thrumming somewhere on the highway,   and I think
now of my couch,   my ceiling,   the steps up the porch,

the door that has to be opened,   the effort this takes,
the going through that hole into another
space I will occupy for the rest of this day

waiting for the next rain,   ground saturated and soft
everything alive,   but thin,   perfect for nutgrass
to spread—   so green it's near purple—   out of control.

Bette Lynch Husted

Balancing the Heart

Life is change. T'ai Chi class: warming up,
shooting the breeze, our teacher
preaching the yin and yang
of pixels. *Face it*, he says.
Paper's obsolete.

We snap our fans. "What? No finger-painting?"
Oh, how we love these swords: red tassels! Thrust and parry.
He sighs, patient, determined.
Your generation—but stops.
We're old: no changing that.

And maddeningly stubborn, holding out for books
the way we do. But it's not books—
their soft pages, their heft—so much as
touch. We've buried lovers.
Boys with brand new driver's licenses.

Watched as children—ours—gasped
through leukemia, graft vs. host. DTs. Last spring
I changed the dressing on his back, this teacher
young enough to be my son. Melanoma.
Stitches like a millipede's black tracks.

So many miles we walked beside our bodies—distant,
polite. Do we have time to learn to feel each bone?
Joints opening and closing, the string of pearls
he talks about? That mystery at the center
balancing the heart?

He smiles. Now we're silk-reeling,
fingertips tasting air. *Remember, breathe.*
Are we playing or praying?
Ride the Tiger. Already
my arms are wings, are purely light.

Valerie Miner

Crossing Back: A Provisional Return

Autumn, 1976

"I am traveling with my eighty-one year old mother," says the man from Trois Rivières.

"Yes?" nods Valery, the taciturn Soviet purser.

"And I would like to know what kind of water she can get in her cabin—Vichy, Perrier, Evian, whatever?"

"In the cabin," the Russian examines the passenger for a minute, then laboriously explains, "We have two kinds of water." Valery sets his jaw, "Hot water and cold water."

It is like this for nine days from London to Montreal on the M.S. Alexandr Pushkin. Not quite the Lillian Hellman adventure I expect. Even Lillian Hellman isn't as Lillian Hellman as she should be when I read her memoirs on board. Her irony turns too suave and the literary gossip becomes too self-conscious. At the age of twenty-nine, I haven't yet learned the secret of ships and old books—let your hopes lead you on, but expect nothing in particular.

§

On this tarted-up Russian ship I was returning—slowly, gradually, reluctantly—to the United States (via a visit to friends in Canada) after almost seven years away. I had left in 1970 in protest against American military action in South East Asia. More American women than men were anti-war expatriates to Canada, something that few people knew then or realize now. I worked as a journalist in Toronto. Four years later, I traveled to London and began to write fiction. I was never going to return to the United States. However, in the months before the Pushkin voyage, several experiences persuaded me to go back to the States for *one year*, to prove to myself I was no longer American. At least that would be one question sorted out. In those days, I regarded contradiction as a character weakness. I boarded the Pushkin with a surfeit of rectitude, a dearth of nuance and an appetite for adventure.

§

Sailing across the Atlantic has a special allure for my post-World War II generation because by the time we start traveling, the only people who take ships are the rich or the rhapsodic. Most people say they don't have time for the ocean. Since 1957, when one million passengers flew between Europe and North America, flights have exceeded sailings. Increasing fuel costs also slow down the shipping industry. The Soviet and Polish lines manage by paying minimal wages and decreasing knots to preserve petrol. Anyway, they're in business more for Western currency than straight profit.

For me the Alexandr Pushkin has both practical and romantic attractions. First it is cheap: $300 compared to a $450 one-way airfare. Also, I have an unfinished feeling about the Soviet Union because in August, 1968, I was in Moscow, headed to Minsk, then Prague. The Soviet troops got to Czechoslovakia first. The U.S. Embassy ordered all American visitors to leave the Soviet Union on the first flight west, thus my Russian chapter was incomplete. From the Pushkin, I expect lectures, *kultur,* conversations about Russia with the crew, answers to some of the questions I never got to ask in 1968.

Of course the crew is busy. Passengers are more ready to talk. They are people like me, who have time, are buying time, are running away from time. Would-be artists and academics returning from their foreign apprenticeships; young European couples expatriating to Canada's higher standard of living; old couples migrating to spend final days in the company of blessed grandchildren; kids going home after six or twelve month odysseys across the Alps or the Sahara turtled in their VW vans. Travelers tired of jet lag and leg cramp. People who need more than eight hours to cross time zones, to exit one life and begin the next.

Like the English woman who tells me about her work in China during the Long March as we sit in her cabin eating Russian liqueur dark chocolates. The Australian motorcyclist in the green beret who never changes his seedy clothes or his motorcycle repair magazine. The young Goan secretary who has found life unsatisfactory in Mombasa and London. The Anglo/French couple returning to Montreal to reform their lives by throwing out the TV and taking siestas. The jeweled, scented Russian lady caked in so much flesh-colored mud and mascara that I wonder if an excavation might reveal Anastasia.

The crew is a somber, silent disappointment. We have little contact with anyone except Vladimir, the Lawrence Welk social director, and Valery, the authoritarian purser. An impasse emerges the first afternoon and solidifies over the next nine days. The Soviets have a set formula for running the ship which does not include idle chat. Even those who can speak English aren't saying much. The formula does include rich meals, Strauss waltzes, bingo, a Mr. and Mrs. Pushkin contest. We are getting a regulation international luxury sailing. No substitutions, please. I try to remember the subsistence salaries; friendliness to the passengers is not part of their job descriptions.

§

It was time to give the U.S. one last try. Amnesty had been granted to war resisters and although I was in no legal danger, I hadn't felt right going back before the men could. I had been gone long enough to grow a new layer of skin. At twenty-nine, I was tilting on a precipice. Soon, according to counterculture sages, I would reach a notably untrustworthy age.

I had been around—reporting from Dar es Salaam on the Summit Conference of liberation leaders from South Africa, Mozambique, Zimbabwe, Namibia. Interviewing Tanzania's President Julius Nyerere, a long time personal hero. Writing about his Ujamaa villages, about women's small industry collectives, the Chinese-built TanZam Railway. In Britain, I reported on men in maximum security lock-up; Scottish gypsies; Lynn Seymour dancing with Rudolf Nureyev at the Royal Ballet. As a reporter in Canada, I covered the trial of Karl Armstrong, an American claiming political refugee status, who was later deported and convicted of bombing the Army-Math Research building in Madison. In Toronto, I also wrote about experimental schools; Native women's land rights; the difficulties faced by Francophones who lived outside Quebec. A decent international track record for a writer in her twenties.

In both Canada and Britain, I was active in anti-war, anti-imperialist and feminist organizations. I learned to call marches "demos." And I did, indeed, start to write fiction. One short story published in a magazine. Three included in a book. None of these stories available in the U.S. I had begun a novel. Would it be real if it never appeared in the window of Cody's Bookstore on Berkeley's Telegraph Avenue? Is this why I was going home—to stand in front of Cody's and look at my book?

§

We board at Tilbury—where the berths are cheaper than those in Southampton—in a brilliant sunset. My housemates have driven me down from North London and they marvel at my wee compartment. Several want to sail with me. (At this point I'm happy to change places. How can I be leaving bustling, cosmopolitan London? Why don't I just ride back to Tufnell Park and let Maggie or Paul sail in my stead? Valerie is an androgynous name on a Russian ship.) The whistle blows and each friend deserts me, hug after hug. Am I going home—or to some irretrievable memory? What am I doing?

That first night, the dining room crackles with nervous cheer. People eye each other for prospective company. Afterward, we explore each other's compact cabins with the joy of children discovering dollhouses. Over the next few days, we continue to marvel at the self-sufficiency of the Pushkin: sauna, gymnasium, ping pong tables, shuttle board, hospital, laundry, tailor shop, games room, music salon, hairdresser, two swimming pools and a library with a plethora of magazines about Soviet Industrial Progress. Still relative strangers, passengers grow closer by congratulating each other—on deck, over dinner, at the bar—on avoiding another bland, uncomfortable plane journey.

Everyone selects a favorite bar. The Rusalka Bar by the swimming pool. The Friendship Bar next to the games room. The Café Penguin or the Café North Palmyra. We listen to stories. The English woman tells how much she yearns to go back to China. Anastasia whispers conspiratorially over semi-precious rings about a Moscow-New York import business. The young Goan asks enthusiastic questions about Canada where her parents plan to find her an educated, Catholic, Brahmin Goan husband somewhere in Toronto's ethernet. The Brisbane motorcyclist haunts the White Knight's bar as he banters obscure Aussie slang with his mate from Melbourne and downs twenty-five cheap Pernods a night. The guy from Melbourne is cute; we exchange arched eyebrows about the drunken biker. Ships are conducive to storytelling. The sea lends time and trust. Besides, after we land, we'll probably never see one another again.

§

In those days I still believed in presenting my resume at each introduction: a professional woman camouflaging the working-class girl. The BBC, *The Guardian*, The New Statesman, *The Economist*, *Time Out*, etc. What I didn't reveal, even after a few too many of those bargain vodkas, were the urgent questions.

Was I lesbian or heterosexual?

Was I a journalist or a fiction writer?

Did I belong in Britain, Canada or the U.S.?

You were supposed to know the answers by the time you were thirty. There was less than a year left.

§

By the fourth day, people have made friends and lovers. (Brian, the guy from Melbourne, and I agree on a low-key affair.) Passengers join classes in the balalaika, the Russian language and folk dancing. From the library I check out a Tolstoy and a Dostoyevsky. The books are good company, but there's nothing like a warm body next to yours to help you fall asleep as you sail into the rest of your life. Brian and I are discreet. This is just a shipboard romance. We don't want the news to travel back home, wherever that may be.

Almost halfway through the voyage, the dollhouse magic is fading away and pampered inmates grow restless. Meals which had once seemed generous, now feel heavy. The Strauss waltzes sound too hardy. Where are those promised "Cultural films?" The English woman and I wonder why the shops with woolen shawls, Matryoshki, fur caps, amber and gold jewelry are closed during afternoon ennui and open during supper hour when we're confined to the dining room. No one complains about the quantity of service, just the spirit. We become aggravated—where yesterday we were amused—

by the maladroit signs, such as this one over the heaters: "It is not permitted, objects to lay on or throw into this unit." There's a turgid disposition, even to the translations.

Hurricane Gloria has a lot to do with the general irritability. We all remember why friends advised us not to sail the Atlantic off season. We drink a little less alcohol, eat a little more Dramamine and try to sleep away the storm. Those of us who get through the night without vomiting don't get much further when we open our doors in the morning and see the corridor railing lined with empty puke bags. Efficient, no doubt, but lacking a certain sensitivity to the power of suggestion.

Forget the Russians and look at the sea. I feel less queasy on deck. And what glory. Brian and I spend an hour watching the ocean splash, toss and curl inside itself. Gleaming waves, tangled like so much foaming seaweed. Brian goes to wake up his biker friend and I stay on alone by the railing, brooding that my cognitive life is a petty circuit of abstraction compared with the immediate force of the ocean. Facing my own frailty in the hurricane, I find freedom in acknowledging that survival is not a simple elective of human will. What are the others thinking about? Captain Ahab? A grandmother left behind in Gdynia? The going price of bathyspheres? People pass by grasping puke bags or deep breathing the salt-fresh air, leaving me to my silent watch.

§

My parents traveled on different ships to distant destinations and it was only when they spent much time in the same port that they realized they were meant to be apart. Mom emigrated from Scotland at age twenty, the illegitimate daughter of prolific parents whose thirteen other impoverished children had already emigrated to New Zealand, India, Australia, British Columbia, Miami, New Haven, Toronto. Dad was a young seaman in the U.S. merchant marine. Eventually my parents met in a New York bar. Voyage was a word learned early by each of their three children. Geography became my favorite subject: Vasco da Gama. Leif Ericson. Ferdinand Magellan. John Miner. Dad was away for much of my childhood, returning every six months or so with fabric from Buenos Aires or photos of Hanoi. He brought his only daughter colorful dolls from Japan and Korea and Holland.

§

Days five and six wash into each other. People doze through the hurricane or page desultorily through their novels. Brian and I discover that seasickness isn't conducive to great sex, but we do find comfort sleeping in each other's arms. What would Tolstoy make of this privileged leisure? Of the waste? Some passengers skip lunch although it seems reckless to sacrifice a whole hour's break in the boredom. My Long March friend and I practice Martha Graham exercises on deck after our folk dancing class. But this only consumes thirty minutes. I'm finding Lillian Hellman increasingly mordant. The thirty-five-cent vodka has begun to taste metallic.

Even the impassive crew members reveal symptoms of glumness, surfacing briefly from circumspection to officiousness. The dour post office clerk refuses to cash Australian travelers' cheques for our shaggy friend in the green beret. He wants to know why she'll cash cheques for the Halifax stockbroker. The stockbroker says it has to do with charm. The clerk says it has to do with currency conversions. The green beret says it has to do with motorcycles. He says it's a matter of class.

§

"Class bias on a Soviet ship?" I ask the Captain.

He has invited me to his cabin. The daughter of another

merchant marine is always welcome, he says.

I see those dolls straining forward to hear our conversation. His office on the top deck smells of shoe polish. The model ship behind his portentous desk rocks back and forth and I look away to avoid another bout of nausea.

He serves brandy to steady my stomach. And caviar. Gleaming hills of caviar. How could something so luscious be bad for me?

Despite his hospitality, the journalist asks her question again. "How can a Soviet ship condone classes?"

The Captain is offended. He looks into my almost-thirty-year-old eyes and smiles with a hint of condescension. "We have no classes. The dining room, the bars, the entertainment: all is open to everyone."

"What about the *grades* of cabin?" The brandy is relaxing. "From bargain basement to spacious boat deck suites?"

"Well," he smiles in a fatherly way, "business is business."

I blink.

"We are building equally commodious ships for Russian passengers, as well."

"But how can a socialist government spend so much on bourgeois comforts?" I smile a little archly.

"The ship is not a ship of the Soviet government, only of the merchant marine. Would you call the Queen Elizabeth II a ship of the Labor government?"

"The QEII is not owned by the state," I say, "but by a capitalist company. Whereas the merchant marine is part of your state...."

He leans forward, interrupting the not-so-dutiful daughter. "Business is business."

§

Business had never appealed to me. Corporations. Companies. Even newsrooms. Early on I chose freelancing. I turned down a graduate fellowship at Columbia Journalism School (which I considered a passport to a good newspaper staff) to become a magazine reporter, eschewing regular paychecks in favor of personal freedom. My first two books were collective efforts. In London, my last job was for the Writers and Readers Publishing Cooperative. I had no retirement fund. And as I left Britain, no health care plan. Still, with almost a year before I turned thirty, almost anything was possible. That was the scary part—almost anything.

§

We sail into clear skies the final few days. The storm has passed. Sunsets go on and on as we travel west away from European time zones. Petty annoyances and political inconsistencies evaporate on the sun-drenched deck and at the Captain's extravagant farewell dinner. Many of us look forward to the evening performance of "The Brothers Karamazov." Finally, a decent film. I hear more resignation than exasperation when Vladimir announces it's in Russian, without subtitles. *What is to be done?* as another Vladimir once asked.

We all rejoice at the glorious purple-scarlet-orange-golden autumn as the Pushkin pushes up the St. Lawrence Seaway. Canadian passengers, bundled in parkas, wave happily to their homeland. I'm a little envious. Could this still be my country? (If I find I really am not American, I dream of Vancouver, where I could live in Canada and still be on the Pacific.) On the bottom deck, crewmembers dance about and peer eagerly through binoculars at the shingled Quebec houses. For many of them, it is the first visit to a land of Levis and milkshakes. I feel sad that we have had such little chance to talk to each other.

§

76

After landing, I would still have a distance to travel before I faced "home" in California. A stopover to see old pals in Toronto. A train across Canada to visit another friend in Edmonton. Then on to Vancouver, where somehow I would find a cheap ride down the coast to San Francisco. My college roommate had offered me a room in the basement of her Berkeley house. I could live on food stamps, she said, even go to the dentist or doctor on the dole until I had a job. Of course I would get a job. I had always had a job.

What I didn't have was a sexuality, a nationality, a profession.

If I didn't discover my identity in the States, I could go back to Vancouver or London. Perhaps Frelimo would accept the application I had submitted to work for the revolution in Mozambique. According to my favorite Tom Gunn poem, "One is always nearer by not keeping still."

§

The last evening is quiet. People are finishing their library books, writing letters, exchanging addresses, packing. The sensible ones go to bed early. Some of us wait on the bridge until we pass Quebec City in the early morning, singing "Alouette." Even the Australians are trying out their Français.

After the song, I stand off to the side, considering the passage of moods. The tears and jubilation of the first nervous night. The regret and anticipation of being away at sea. Fear, then aggravation, then boredom provoked by Hurricane Gloria. Good cheer when we finally sail into sun. I recall my tenacious hold on that first sighting of land. I feel a vigor being back in Canada, a land I once thought was the answer to all my questions before my questions multiplied. Now I anticipate the melancholy of docking, saying farewell to Brian, watching my nine-day-chums disappearing into a crowd of spouses, siblings and friends.

Perhaps there is one inimitably Russian mood—a sense of

77

irresolution. If you take the Pushkin with worthy internationalist intentions, you land frustrated by the cautious crew, disappointed in the polemical periodicals and kitsch programs. However, accepting the impasse, you are grateful for whatever Russian sensibility has been incidentally revealed. In that way, a trip on the Pushkin is like a visit to the Soviet Union. Always an unfinished business.

§

Postscript: I stay longer than a year. One month laps into another; one decade into the next. I write this essay from my cabin in the Mendocino Hill Country, a cabin I share with Helen, my partner of thirty years. Since that trip on the Pushkin, I've published eleven books of fiction and two books of nonfiction. Although I've lived much of the intervening thirty-four years in the U.S., I have spent considerable periods away in India, Australia, England, Scotland, Norway and other countries.

When I recall the intense young writer on the Pushkin, I feel bemused by her earnestness, impressed with her courage and grateful for her openness. An immigrant's daughter, she immigrated back to the country her mother adopted. She turned out to be a reluctant American. You might say she became—not capricious, exactly—but someone with a taste for contradiction.

What happened to my fellow voyagers? I imagine my Long March friend made at least one more trip to China after the Cultural Revolution. (I think of her when I, myself, walk along the Great Wall in 1983.) I can see the Australian motorcyclist running an Antipodean automobile empire. Our Captain must have retired to a comfortable *dacha* free of troubling questioners. After *Glasnost,* the purser probably started a designer water business. I hope the Goan found lasting romance in Canada. I know that Brian found lice—because I couldn't stop scratching by the time I reached Edmonton.

Dorianne Laux

Dark Charms

Eventually the future shows up everywhere:
burly summers and unslept nights in deep
lines and dark splotches, thinning skin.
Here's the corner store grown to a condo,
the bike reduced to one spinning wheel,
the ghost of a dog that used to be, her trail
no longer trodden, just a dip in the weeds.
The clear water we drank as thirsty children
still runs through our veins. Stars we saw then
we still see now, only fewer, dimmer, less often.
The old tunes play and continue to move us
in spite of our learning, the wraith of romance,
lost innocence, literature, the death of the poets.
We continue to speak, if only in whispers,
to something inside us that longs to be named.
We name it the past and drag it behind us,
bag like a lung filled with shadow and song,
dreams of running, the keys to lost names.

Jan Eliot

No Offense, Mom

Kelly Cherry

Lines Written on the Eve of a Birthday

It is the loss of possibility
That claims you bit by bit. They take away
Your man, the children you had hoped would be,
They even take brown hair and give you gray
Instead. You ask if you can save your face
But that is part of their plan—to strip you
Of your future and put the past in its place.
They don't stop there. They take the skies' deep blue
And drain it off; the empty bowl they leave
Inverted, white as bone. They dust the trees
With strontium, but they keep up their sleeve
The biggest trick of all, the one that sees
     You give up in the end. It is the loss
     Of possibility that murders us.

Alexandra Marshall

Phrases of Movement

Centuries before Freud's proclamation about anatomy and destiny, Venus and Mars inspired the ♀ and ♂ gender symbols—a hand mirror or a shield and spear—by which we abbreviate female and male reproductive organs with a circle or a line. Acknowledging the oversimplification, we accept the basic characterization of men as linear and women as circular, while noting the obvious contradiction that, despite their cyclical nature, women generally outlive their childbearing years.

Because I repeated Biology One, I discovered—and rediscovered!—a form of reproduction called mitosis, where a mother cell's nucleus divides to form a daughter. In the meantime, of course, I'd also picked up the basics concerning human reproduction, but I didn't let this more complex knowledge diminish the awesome example of microscopic jade-tinted matter reproducing by forming itself into buds that split off like succulents.

Even to an eighth-grader in a pre-feminist era, it was the ultimate in self-reliance to possess such a powerful nucleus, and while I knew better than to wish to have been born a single-cell vegetable instead of the white middle-class American girl that I was, the concept of such radical independence was alluring. What would it be like to enjoy such solitary creativity? I wondered about this a lot more than anybody knew.

I was in my late 20s before I would officially define myself as a writer, but in having been the precocious proprietor of a secret diary, I'd already claimed the power of reproduction. The little girl who existed only on the page—under lock and key in the experimental cursive of a preteen—was as independent a being as any fictional character I've since created. A far sharper observer than I, she dared to tell people off in all the ways I wasn't allowed to. Not having to suffer the relationship between actions and their consequences, she could hate without having to love at the same time. She could love without fear of rejection. What freedom she enjoyed!

Isn't it the definition of a diary to be both that empty vessel seeking fulfillment and that handheld mirror reflecting a version of what already is?

§

Abandoning science (and vice versa), I had meanwhile found my passionate way, on the first try, into the brave new worlds of French and Modern Dance. Team sports were such the focus in my elite all-girls school that the entire population was divided into blue or red—combining to make purple, the school color—with the fortunate option for an artsy minority to satisfy the requirement while wearing the dancer's black uniform of a leotard and barefoot tights. We "expressed ourselves" in that mirrored basement sanctuary, but it counted as gym.

Similarly, in those remaining few years before JFK read *The Ugly American* and rushed to commission the Peace Corps, the study of a foreign language was more about qualifying for college than any effort to expand horizons. And while I won't pretend that the irregular verbs were any less daunting for me than for every other student of entry-level French, I can still recall the active sensation of escaping the known confines of my native language. Soon, French became an invitation to journey into the exotic other of The Romantic Poets whose work was at once succinct and melodramatic.

83

And it would even prove possible—*et voilà!*—to choreograph dances inspired by that dark imagery.

It was a short leap to France itself, but, except for two summer jobs in Paris during college, I cast my lot with the culture that had invented the American form of dance called Modern. Taught in a serious way at my women's college and augmented with studies at a nearby conservatory, I pursued dance like a stalker, giving it my best energies despite a full academic load. When the phrases of movement piled up like paragraphs, I convinced other dancers to hear the music that echoes in the silence—the white space, on the page—when the transition is imprecise. With Martha Graham my muse, I explored pagan themes. Rather than by Disney's "Fantasia" creation myth, by way of Graham's anti-ballet interpretation of *Le Sacre du Printemps* with the ritual sacrifice of a young girl—death by dancing—I too found Stravinsky.

§

From there my travels brought me to Kyoto for an extended detour, where I was initiated into a formal study of Japanese classical dance and introduced to the language I would further struggle to learn, back home. While diverging, I was conscious of the natural way these new interests formed an overlapping circle with my first two loves. But since I'd meanwhile married, it seemed more practical to return to French for a graduate program that included teacher certification.

Perhaps this linear lapse prepared me for the far less considered leap I made one year later when I took up writing, although at the time I understood my sudden shift as the logical substitution of fiction writing for my proven devotion to dance and French. It even pleased me to think that with this new pursuit I was blending the other two—red and blue into purple—as if all along I'd been seeking the simplicity of unification. The more urgently compelling truth was that, at a literal crossroads after my 28-year-old husband's suicide while we were on assignment with Operation Crossroads Africa, my life had been simultaneously thrown wide open and clamped shut.

So I was "moving on" by not persisting with the disciplines I'd been trained in, and while it seemed like a coherent maneuver to reinvent myself as a writer by recycling my skills as a choreographer and a linguist, wasn't I also depriving myself of the very positive reinforcement by which I'd been sustained? Having identified dance and French as the life preservers I'd clung to in order to stay afloat during adolescence, why throw myself into deeper waters?

§

I did it anyway. Joining the daily grind of voluntary self-employment while living on modest savings and a minimal life-insurance settlement, I wrote three practice novels in five years. Making everything up as I went along, I found my way onto slush piles and eventually into the actual hands—the grip—of publishing. Within a mere seven years of downward mobility and a fourth "first" novel under contract, I'd finally arrived, at the start.

The gift that came with this changed way of life was the immense solitude that proved to be a consolation while I "lived with" death. A quieter life with a single goal suited me, I found, and it's possible that I regained my balance in part by reconnecting with that brash preteen girl who kept journals. With my first publication I felt not only validated but recovered—retrieved—and while I consciously regretted losing my fluency in language and dance, I gradually resumed a more inclusive life with a happy remarriage and the births of my children.

Setting my gaze on the straightaway, I could afford to ignore the rearview mirror for a change as I continued to quietly write my quiet novels. I taught on the side and threw in my opinion with a range of essays, gradually realizing a mid-level of vocational fulfillment that I had the wisdom and the grace not to take for granted. Yet whenever I was asked to speak at a school or a college, I'd urge students to take note of their current interests and talents and look for ways to intersect these skills. As if the purpose of an education is to recombine it. As if the point of a life is to learn to make lemonade.

§

Any series of reflections on aging will naturally include among its themes the losses endured, including perhaps a lamentable accumulation of them as we move beyond our middle years. In my own case, as I age, I've become increasingly alert to what I suffered young, with the abrupt loss of my husband quickly followed by the illness and death of my mother. This is why I return to the puzzle of how it was that in a state of crisis I fled the familiar, when the risk in further undermining my fragile sense of self was to intensify the grief that already defined me. It's entirely possible that a natural function of loss is the generation of more loss, but I still wonder why I would give up my cherished fluency in dance and French to "start over" as if I were just starting out.

The simplest answer is that the horrible story compelled me to tell it. Indeed, the first thing I wrote was called *Child Widow*, a surreal version of the trauma that I would persist in imagining and re-imagining, never quite aligning my narrative with the whole truth. Not even a 30th anniversary return to Africa prompted a successful novel, and though I relentlessly sought publication for these alternate scenarios, I finally collapsed all that unrequited energy into the writing of a short story, my first, which I also called "Child Widow" with the firm intent to close that chapter at last. Its appearance in *Ploughshares* earned a mention among "100 Other Distinguished Stories" in that year's *Best American Short Stories* to further encourage me—The End—to abandon further efforts to fictionalize those events. As I have.

§

Meanwhile, a perpendicular shift was set in motion when, more than a decade ago, I renewed contact with a close friend from college whose double commitment to dance and French, unlike mine, had remained as such. That is, with her French major she too had gone on to grad school, but while keeping her French alive she'd also pursued the more disciplined and rigorous training that would allow her to claim dance for her profession. Soon making her home at the Alvin Ailey American Dance Theater, new at the time, she would spend the entirety of her career as The Ailey School's renowned and beloved director, preparing generations of dancers that include nearly 90% of the present Company. With Denise Jefferson's death occurring exactly a year ago, I am all the more grateful for the impulse I had to tell *her* story.

It was my first visit to the Ailey headquarters then located in a warehouse building west of Lincoln Center, and I made my way down the linoleum corridor to the director's office by sidestepping a herringbone pattern of the extended legs of her students warming up for class. My observation of Denise's workday began with the next ninety minutes reminding me, in my bones, of the way it was once possible for me too to move from one combination to the next, organically building the elements of a familiar technique into a linked chain of steps. A drummer kept the pulse she set, and as the dancers exerted themselves under her instruction, the wall-to-wall windows gradually steamed up to become opaque.

Observantly coaxing her students to get the results she wanted, Denise set the example with a dancer's body I recognized from decades before, when she was a college freshman encountering Modern for the first time after years as an ambitiously focused student of Classical Ballet. Her connection with the rigorous technique of Martha Graham was solidified with her discovery that, in this distinctly American dance form, race wasn't the barrier she'd been up against in that older, Eurocentric tradition. Here, there were role models with footsteps to follow in. And with Denise's experience of Alvin Ailey's genius as a choreographer, she too had a showcase.

As I accompanied her that day from class to class and meeting to meeting, I was as absorbed in the details of her work as if it were my own. With a colleague on the Ailey faculty she was commissioning a new academic program in conjunction with Fordham University, a BFA to provide Ailey dancers with a back-up plan for the notoriously demanding profession they'd chosen. Once again setting the example, this time in how to balance more than one pursuit, every one of the students she selected for the program would succeed in realizing their first dreams.

And what else was she up to? Well, in addition to serving on too many boards and committees, she had a pet project on the island of Guadeloupe that she'd been involved in from the start, an annual *Semaine de la Danse* culminating in a competition for young dancers from around the Caribbean Basin, whose winners would advance to compete at the national level, in Paris.

§

My profile of Denise Jefferson appeared as the cover story in *The Boston Globe Magazine* but, in having followed her to Guadeloupe to observe her at work in that alternative setting, the lasting impact of my tagging along was that it initiated my own commitment to making an annual visit with her for *La Semaine de la Danse*.

How it made us laugh to find ourselves speaking French again—to each other!—nearly a half-century after we sat together at the seminar tables where it always felt slightly ridiculous for pairs of Americans to pretend to be at the Sorbonne when we were so obviously in Massachusetts. Though she and I had clearly both lost something of the facility, with the advantage of age it mattered less and less whether the vocabulary was intact, and more and more not to have lost it altogether. Not even I had relinquished it, despite having willfully left it behind in the mistaken belief that less could be more. In fact, I regained it so efficiently, and so naturally, that it was as if it had never been absent from me.

Back in college, where the academic was kept separate from the extracurricular, there was no chance to combine the two, but with these hundreds of little Francophone dancers in Guadeloupe there wasn't a choice. In their diligent company I knew better than to think my own long-gone identity as a dancer was even remotely salvageable, and yet—abstractly—it somehow felt like it was.

It was at least a partial recovery of the girl I'd been and the young woman I'd lost along the way—in my conscious attempt *not* to lose her—as well as a healing, welcome act of circling back, however belatedly. But because I was to find that dance and French mattered as much as ever, I also had a new question to ask myself. How on earth could I ever have imagined I wouldn't miss them?

Leigh Anne Jasheway

Facing Facts

Occasionally I think about having my face done. I don't know how or when my face came undone—but these days when I look in the mirror I see a gorgeous twenty-something babe until I put on my glasses; then Phyllis Diller is staring back at me. I've started taking long steamy showers to fog over the mirror so I don't have to look her in the eye.

I just got the hot water bill, though, and think maybe having a little "work" done might be a cheaper alternative. This despite the fact that whenever I hear anyone talking about having work done on her face, I conjure up the image of a tiny construction crew jackhammering and laying asphalt, with signs warning "Eyelids falling!" or "Jowls in road!"

Today, Phyllis and I had a free consultation with an Aesthetic Surgeon. The word "aesthetic" is from the Greek meaning "one who makes payments on his Lexus by lowering your self-esteem." Sure enough, when I got to the clinic there were three Lexuses (or is that Lexi?) parked out front. Pulling into the parking lot in my beat-up old Honda helped prepare me for the jolt to my self-esteem that was to come.

Once inside, I was greeted by a lovely young woman with a face so tight and wrinkle-free it chirped against her cheekbones when she spoke. She welcomed me and gave me a form to fill out.

Question #1: Why are you here? I thought about telling them about Phyllis and how she popped up every time I caught my reflection in windows or soup spoons. But I didn't want them to think that in addition to having my face fixed, I needed to have my head examined. So I answered with "Objects in mirror can't possibly be as old as they appear."

Question #2: What kind of results do you expect? I don't expect miracles, but surely it wouldn't be too much to hope that I could look like Reese Witherspoon or Beyoncé, right?

Question #3: Who is responsible for payment? I wanted to say "Whoever drove here today in a Lexus," but I was afraid they wouldn't go for that arrangement, so I put down "Mom." After all, this is probably her fault.

As soon as I finished my form, another stunning young woman escorted me to the examining room and asked me to sit in a large black leather chair. I was hoping it might have a built-in massager so I could reduce the stress I was starting to feel, but no such luck. Instead it had a spotlight aimed directly at it. As I reached for my sunglasses, the doctor came in and handed me a mirror. That's when I figured out what the spotlight was for. You know how they have special lighting in jewelry stores to make the diamonds sparkle? Well, the spotlight had its own "special" purpose—to make you look as bad as humanly possible. In that harsh light, it looked as if the dark circles under my eyes went all the way to my knees. I've seen fewer wrinkles on raisins. My pores were so large grizzlies could have hibernated in them.

"So, what'd you have in mind?" the doctor asked politely. "A face transplant?" I said jokingly. He mumbled something about how important it was to do this kind of thing while still youngish (I put the emphasis on the "young," not the "ish"). He suggested a few procedures that could help me look "refreshed." First, Botox to smooth out a few frown lines; then some collagen injections around my mouth, and laser resurfacing of my whole face. The total price would come to around $1,200, and it would all have to be redone every three months or so. After all, who needs a retirement plan?

91

I politely said I would study my options, and then I ran outside. When I got into the natural light and saw my reflection in the window of the Lexus I had parked closest to, I noticed Phyllis was gone and I suddenly looked much younger and more attractive. All without having had any "work" done at all.

So here's what I'm going to do. The next time Ms. Diller pops up, I'm going to schedule another free consultation. Apparently, there's something about staring into that glaring hot spotlight that scares her away.

Fax Sinclair

Images of Aging

Mardi Gras

Cindy & Billy

Muzza Love

Sixty

Susan M. Tiberghien

"The Riches of a Season"

May Sarton wrote in *Journal of a Solitude*, "I think of trees and how simply they let go, let fall the riches of a season, and go deep into their roots for renewal and sleep." Sarton wrote this when she was 58. I am soon 78. The riches of a season speak to me still more strongly.

With age, we have time to choose what we look at. I look at trees. How they reach both upward and downward. How each year their leaves fall and go deep into their roots. The maple trees that I can see from my front door, across the park, turn bright crimson each fall. This is a rare treat for an American in Switzerland where there are not many maple trees. I walk under them and look up at the leaves, awed by the different shades of red against blue sky.

When the leaves start to fall, I choose a few to take home, each with its five lobes in place. They take me by the hand, back to memories of my childhood—to sitting high in leafy trees and dreaming of faraway places, to playing in piles of autumn leaves, kicking them up in the air and watching them settle back on the ground. I write about them, letting them teach me to hold on to my dreams and then to settle back on the ground.

My maple leaves also have pitch black tar spots. When I was a child and collected leaves to dip into melted wax and put in albums, I used to try to scrape off the tar spots. But I only tore apart the leaves. I learned to wax also the spots. The pitch black and the bright red. As an adult, I fell in love, had a large family, traveled far.

The colors were bright. I saw abuse, experienced violence, nursed illness close-up. The spots were dark. Today, I look at the bright red.

The maple trees show me how to accept the transience of life and gather the riches of each season. To love the springtime, when the primroses poke their heads out of the dark earth and the pear trees soon blossom into white flowers. To slow down in summer and listen to birdsong in late afternoon. To wait for autumn when the maple trees catch fire, and the leaves fall and return to their roots. And to welcome winter. There is time to rest. Time to sleep. It's all right. I know that spring is around the corner.

These are the riches of the seasons when I accept my own finitude, when I accept that I too will go deep into my roots. Then aging gives me time to look at the maple trees with awe. To live in rhythm with the seasons, welcoming each one. And to give thanks for my husband, my children, and for my grandchildren, those wonderful little bodies of energy, teaching me that the love I give will continue to flourish.

Hester L. Furey

House of Mercy

Into a glass each day
she poured her house of mercy.
Each day she did it
until the bone house
she danced in crumbled.
First she broke her leg.
Then her brain stopped.
Then her colon.

Another mother
sat in her garage
breathing in exhaust,
her own last poem.
Her safety glass walls
had always been breached.
The relentless clicks
made their way to her
like water torture;
she had to end it,
cheated, the priests said.
We have been expelled.

One ancestor, both
lucky and wise, who

had the providence
to build a country
in his heart, peopled
it with romance: the
glory of old fools
who lived well, courtly
love, earthly magic,
revolutionaries,
austere and kind, and
the gay art lovers,
resurrectionists
who build worlds again,
who show us how to
outlive our troubles.
Long he dwelled among
them, in his green home,
spent a lot of time
fixing it up, then
left it to the public,
real noblesse oblige.

With me it was books.
I made walls around
me, dove into the
stream of words and left,
vanishing through that
portal, every day,
hours, years, decades gone,
until, eyes become
flaming swords, I heard
Enough. Turn back now.
Back to the painful
body I'd ignored

I came raging like
a child, my skin still
tender, abraded
from that second birth.
Everywhere the judge
calls to my thieving soul
like the rooster in the tale,
"bring the rascal to me!"
I have to live here,
in these guts, these bones.
My house, my garden
lie open to storms,
drought, all the whims of
passing clouds. Only
the earth and water
deliver mercy,
receive me in grace;
I am transmuted,
there, like a seed, or,
become butterfly
instantly, or worm,
with no memory
of the difference.

Clare MacQueen

Photo by Gary Gibbons

The Fragrance of Levity

I. *"Neither the sun nor death can be looked at steadily."* [1]

You and Gary lean against each other. The silence is palpable, the floor apparently empty on a Sunday afternoon. Where are the patients? He tells you later the place was "dead quiet" and you know Kelley would have snickered with him over that one. Michelle the charge nurse appears and says things are ready, so you follow her down the hallway. Outside the impromptu viewing room, she warns that tracheal and nasal tubes used during CPR are still in place.

"I'm so sorry," she says. "You're sure you want to do this?"

"Yes," you say, wishing for one more chance to talk with Kelley, one more chance to hug her and say I love you. With a deep breath, you step forward. *Be thou not afraid, for lo, I am always with thee.* This phrase has steadied you many times since your daughter's birth. Gary steps into the room behind you and stops, while Michelle stations herself outside. You hesitate and then walk resolutely around the privacy curtain—and everything stops. Your lungs, your heart, even the clock freezes while the scene sears ghost images onto your retinas.

And then everything resumes again, savagely. *Oh Jesus and Mary and all the bodhisattvas of heaven!* It really is your child in that bed. Or it used to be. The bed is like those in any other hospital room, waist high with head elevated for easier access, but it's clear this person no longer needs nursing. The light of your life has flickered out.

Oh Kelley, my sweet brown-eyed girl!

She lies on her back, ashen and pale, arms at her sides beneath a white sheet which covers her naked body up to her chin. Tubes trail down her face, one of them forcing her mouth open. You gasp and cry quietly as you softly touch her right shoulder, her cheek, her hair. With trembling lips, you kiss her forehead but her skin is cold and gray. Her essence left this body hours ago. The blood has long since drained from her lips. They look unnatural, a light bronze color as if tattooed with a ghastly face powder. Strangely, her eyes are half open.

You lift the sheet and notice bruises beneath her body from her neck and shoulders down past her calves. *Who did this?!* You want to scream, you want to roar blood and brimstone, you want to crush testicles and bash a selfish skull. But you caution yourself that CPR may have caused this trauma. Looking at Kelley's ribcage, you see no bruising there, no bones protruding. Still, best to collect more evidence before burning her ex-boyfriend at the stake of misplaced furies. With heart pounding, you place your hand on your chest and breathe deeply.

After moving to the other side of the bed, you kiss Kelley's forehead again. *I'm so sorry, my sweet girl, so sorry.* You mindlessly stroke her hair, lifting the cold strands in each hand. Gary gasps and you look up to see him standing across from you. You were unaware he had walked around the curtain himself. He turns his head away and his shoulders jerk.

"Sweetie, you don't have to do this," you say, as anguished for him as you are for Kelley and yourself.

"Yes I do," he says. "I'm here for your sake." He wipes his face with a tissue and you follow suit, grateful that you both thought to fill your pockets before leaving the car.

Michelle rustles beyond the doorway so you resume your inspection. Resting your fingertips on Kelley's shoulder, you lift the sheet with your other hand to check her left side. The bruising is here, too, though less extensive. And it's a strange color on both sides, not black or blue or green, but a pale mottled rose. The blush of anemia? Such odd contusions, you think. But then you have never seen a corpse this close before, much less one refrigerated for 16 hours. How can you know what to expect?

As you move toward the foot of the bed, you lift and drop the sheet gently while sweeping your eyes along Kelley's body. You see no other obvious signs of trauma. A defibrillator patch adheres to her chest. A mesh IV bandage encircles her left wrist. Her toenails sport a neon shade of fuchsia, one of your favorite colors in the garden. No wear at the tips so she probably painted them yesterday.

You consider rolling her body toward Gary, to check for injuries along her back, but all at once you think, *Enough!* There's nothing more you can do to protect her. Ever again. Your throat constricts even as you also realize your daughter is no longer in pain, no longer afraid, no longer suffering. Clutching this one comfort, you drop the sheet for the last time and give in to mourning. Gary rushes to wrap himself around you. He cradles your head against his shoulder and you cling to him in return, afraid of losing him, too.

"Oh Clare," he cries, "oh Sweetie!" and sobs along with you.

II. *"Hope is the refusal to accept things as they are."* [2]

Laundry is your favorite chore. You like to treat the coffee stains, check pockets for spare change, turn shirts right-side-out. And folding clothes warm from the dryer is meditative, a perfect way to practice mindfulness. How Kelley hates to fold clothes! Hated, you correct yourself. It occurs to you that not only has she passed from one plane of existence to another, but she's also switched tenses. She might appreciate that.

"What's another word for synonym?" she once asked.

"What?" you said. "Hey, that's brilliant. How do you think of these things?"

"I borrowed that one from my homeboy George," she confessed with a chortle.

How can she be gone? You miss her profoundly. Who will call you "hairless Chihuahua" now as she complains about shaving her legs? Who will threaten to pick your tiny blackheads after you get Alzheimer's and can no longer fend her off? Who will entertain you with lines from *Forrest Gump* and *My Big Fat Greek Wedding*?

And who will appreciate your pitiful imitations in return: *Oh why, Kelley?* *"Why you want to leave me?!"*

One day fifty years ago, as you ran barefoot through fields near your home, you accidentally stomped on a sticker-burr. Dry and sharp, it hurt. You knew how to extract the tiny stickers and be on your way again. But on that particular day, the pain of that particular burr was more than you could bear. You collapsed on your back in the sandy soil and began to wail. Raising your foot skyward, you cried, "Please God, take it out!" And God did. You raise your eyebrows at such stories now, but at the age of six you believed. God simply was, just as the rain you loved simply was. Whether the burr fell out on its own, you will never know. But they typically embed their barbs in tender skin, especially under the weight of running feet. And you were alone in that field.

A fifty-year-old dream then? Moon's reflection on water? One illusion amongst many that comprise your reality? You enjoy speculating like this but would rather believe in a benevolent and compassionate creator. In fact, you have sent this deity many prayers since you were a child. Yet you were struck by disconnection on the way home from the hospital. Kelley's presence was utterly gone. For several frightening minutes, you felt severed and *alone*, an alien sensation given that solitude is your nature. But this was spiritual blindness—your conduit to the divine itself had disappeared. *Dear God, please help me!* Yet none of your prayers and mantras were working. You felt unprotected and mortal as panic prowled your body. You tried to relax, tried to anchor your mind to something tangibly sacred, like the mountains that cradle Puget Sound and offer such glorious scenery on sunny evenings. Gary reached over to hold your hand, a habit of his while driving. You squeezed back gratefully with both hands, and like a squall the panic soon passed.

Yet Kelley is still gone, and you're uncertain about matters of the spirit. You expected clarity by now—with age comes wisdom—yet your vision seems cloudier than ever. You see decay and death everywhere. Honey bees drop in mid-flight, their wondrous wings tattered, having worked themselves to death to ensure the hive's survival. Yet new bees continuously emerge from pupation to replace them. Spent blossoms wilt in the garden, melting into the soil even as new buds open in the sunlight. You try to reframe loss, to understand it not as annihilation but as transition from one state of being to another. Change is the basic currency of life, you know this. Why waste precious energy raging against the inevitable? And why wrestle with your own mortality? Everything dies! Yet you drag your fearful bones through swampland, struggling to balance acceptance and despair. Damn it all, you kept hoping she could change.

Kelley was in and out of clinics and emergency rooms and hospitals countless times during her adult life. Mainly to treat panic attacks and minor injuries that escalated in severity and frequency. Beginning with her hand, broken after she jumped off the roof of the laundry room beside her first apartment. She misplaced her keys during a night of partying and tried to leap from roof to deck, planning to slip inside the unlocked door. Unfortunately, miscalculation landed her on the concrete below. Incredulous that she broke nothing else, you bombarded her guardian angels with prayers of thanksgiving. Not that you actually believed in angels with wings, but why not cover the bases? And if such creatures do exist, she kept a team of them busy.

A few years later, she broke the same hand again. It was repaired then with a metal plate and screws, producing an ache that never went away. After weeks of physical therapy, she returned to work at Canlis Restaurant, where she balanced heavy plates of haute cuisine on each arm while negotiating stairs between kitchen and dining areas. Her wicked wit and charm, her subtle skill at upselling, her ability to spin the stories her guests wanted to hear—all these helped her reel in astonishing tips and generate six-figure revenues for Canlis. One night she received a $600 tip at one table alone, though she was obligated to share it with support staff. Eight years of this part-time work left Kelley disillusioned and with fulltime pain in her shoulders and neck.

Two years ago, her other hand became infected after a bite from one of the dogs her ex-boyfriend owns. Surgery relieved the swelling and reduced the risk of nerve damage. She called you with the news, impressed that her surgeon had said her swollen hand looked as if it had been run over by a truck. Uncharitably, you wondered whether it was Rob's van instead.

"Oh Mom, of course not!" she said. "I got in the way between two pups playing rough, that's all. Anyone who lives with dogs gets bitten sooner or later."

You weren't so sure that's what happened, but you let it go.

And then there was the bruised hip from tripping on stairs at Rob's house.

The cracked rib from another fall down the same stairs.

The toe she fractured twice in one year.

The upper lip supposedly clawed by a neighbor's cat as it tried to escape a barking dog.

Plus, a multiplicity of illnesses, including cysts, recurrent and painful endometriosis, and pelvic infections that required round after round of antibiotics because Rob refused treatment himself. He insisted he wasn't infected despite the fact that men typically show no symptoms of this disease. So he continued to re-infect her while accusing her of unfaithfulness. Such ignorance and selfishness you could not fathom, nor the fact that she kept returning to someone who treated her that way. You wanted to educate him, but she and

Gary made you promise not to confront Rob yourself. His denials not only hurt her emotionally but led also to the pain of pelvic scarring, which led in turn to hysterectomy. And he had other commitments the day of that surgery. So you drove down to Seattle to hug her and assure her that everything would be all right.

And everything was, until MRSA attacked her incisions afterward. It took three more hospital stays to vanquish the infection, one you believed was inevitable for someone who spent so much time in emergency rooms. Hospitals are hazardous places, filled with malignant microbes and mistakes waiting to happen. But you refrained from harping. Why inflame her anxieties further?

The incisions took months to heal, but your own wounds still weep. Hysterectomy! Kelley was your only child, the one you thought would carry into the next generation your legacy and your mother's before you. You grieve that you will never share the joys of reading with your grandchildren, never act goofy with them, never kiss their cheeks and pamper them, even as you understand this could be a blessing. Was she too sick for motherhood? She had said she didn't want children anyway, at least not Rob's. But though she was silent after the surgery, you think she too mourned the loss on some level. It's only natural.

III. *"For what is it to die but to stand naked in the wind and to melt into the sun?"* [3]

Aging expands the vocabulary. With every move it seems, you and Gary grunt and groan with new inflections. Climbing stairs, getting in and out of the car, pulling on a sweater. No more wild love on the kitchen table. Your hips ache too much afterward.

Pondering, you sit and look with tenderness at the skin inside your forearm. Beneath its translucent stipples and crinkles, a blue-green vein runs prominently from wrist to crook of elbow. When and how did this skin become so fragile-looking? And how long before it begins to bruise spontaneously, like your mother's during her last years? How long before these newly developing freckles blossom into age spots? Bleeding beneath your skin concerns you because you're anemic already, but spots hardly faze you. Pregnancy bestowed pigmentation upon the left side of your neck from jaw to collarbone. San Diego sunshine first darkened this discoloration thirty-one summers ago, leaving your neck looking dirty in a lopsided way ever since, as if you forgot to wash after playing in the dust. But you will never lighten this skin or conceal it with cosmetics as advised by nurses you've known. This hormonal mask symbolizes your most important achievements: incubating, birthing, and nurturing the child you will forever carry close to your heart.

Just as your silken wrinkles signify your good fortune to have loved and laughed for half-a-century. You're officially an antique and proud that your face proves it. Having yearned for them since your twenties, you celebrate your crow's feet especially. Laugh lines are lovely on most any face.

Michelle's beauty was undeniable yet her face was unmarked and therefore unremarkable. "May I have a band-aid?" you asked. As Gary drove to the hospital, you had distractedly pulled at a cuticle. Your finger still oozed blood. "Of course," she said, producing one. Then she eased papers in front of you and gave you a pen.

Finger bandaged, you filled in the time as 4:09 p.m. before signing for Kelley's possessions. "I'd like to see her," you said, your voice tentative. "Is that possible?"

Michelle hesitated, said she needed to check with her manager, and hurried off.

"Are you sure?" Gary asked.

"I need to touch her," you said. "Otherwise, this isn't real." You understood the necessity even as you recoiled from it. How would you know Kelley had actually died, until you saw her body with your own eyes?

Gary suggested taking her belongings to the car in the meantime, so the two of you wheeled them out on a cart. He hefted the suitcase twice—"Must weigh fifty pounds!"—before figuring out how to maneuver the monstrosity into the Malibu's trunk. Next came a large backpack, a shoulder bag, and a purse, each stuffed so full you marveled that she could lug around such weight. At 5'8" your daughter was a tall woman, as tall as your mother was, but this was at least a hundred pounds of baggage.

Not counting the hospital bags. Two contained clothing Kelley wore when she was admitted, including a soft burgundy scarf which you instinctively raised to your face. To your disappointment, it smelled like stale disinfectant. The third bag held magazines and books, including two by George Carlin and one by David Sedaris, her favorite comedians. You gave her the Sedaris book for her birthday three summers ago, and four years before that, surprised her with tickets to hear him perform in Seattle. You both guffawed while reading passages aloud from these books and other favorites. The muscles of your belly, your ribcage, and your cheeks ached after such merriments.

How did you fail to notice when the laughter between you stopped?

IV. *"For life and death are one, even as the river and the sea are one."* [4]

Despite the hysterectomy, her pelvic pain continued, along with mysterious internal bleeding which caused anemia so severe she received transfusions. Ulcers, you speculated. Long-term use of painkillers can burn tiny sores into tissues whose ravaged capillaries leak away a person's vitality. Yet endoscopy and colonoscopy results were inconclusive.

"Gotta drink a whole glass of water with those things," you reminded her. This teetered between helping and meddling, but this was life and death. Yet she continued to chase pills with only a gulp or two of water. Weary of your worries, she said, "I'll be fine, Mom."

Of course you worried. You had lived and learned too much not to, though you grappled with letting go. After all, you preferred not to meddle. She was an adult and, goodness knows, you longed to live a quiet life. You wanted her to make her own choices even as you hoped to protect her from self-destruction. How best to do that? Preferring the middle way of moderation, you practiced a measure of tough love for 15 years. You refused to buy or lend her money for cigarettes, alcohol, or prescription painkillers. And you didn't bail her out. Not seven years ago after she sideswiped a parked car, got arrested for DUI, and spent a night in jail. And not four summers ago when she was sentenced to thirty days in jail after failing to appear for a third DUI hearing. That confinement was hellish for you both, yet it seemed to teach her what you had hoped for: that her ability to charm her way out of trouble had limits, and there were serious consequences to breaking laws designed to protect us all.

You hoped this wisdom was a step toward moderation in her life. And when she ran low on cash, you bought vitamins and organic foods to nourish her beleaguered body. You visited her in rehab, both times. You coached her through panic attacks and encouraged her to manage these episodes herself rather than burden overworked emergency-room staff. You urged her to join support groups, researching phone numbers and addresses because she had no internet access and no bus fare to the library.

And Gary bought her an expensive set of quilted, lavender-infused wraps from the mall. The largest draped across her aching neck and shoulders like a soothing shawl, providing relief whether microwaved or frozen. Kelley wore her fragrant "shawl" so often it soon needed a good washing. But soap and water would ruin the herbs within, so the wrap grew grimy with oil and sweat.

The last day you saw her was nine weeks before her death. You remember her face was gray. Even Gary said she looked sick. You remember she rarely laughed anymore. She no longer surprised you with quips to make you giggle. In fact, you hadn't seen her smile in ages. It broke your heart she was always fatigued, always in pain, always suffering anguish of one kind or another.

You yourself had felt exhausted for years, with your frustrations and impotence regenerating like blackberry brambles despite periodic pruning. You began to despair that Kelley would ever get better. Or could ever take care of you in your dotage. You began to resent her illnesses and surgeries, her latest encampment on your couch in a crowded house, the weeks of listening to her snore and struggle to breathe as muscle relaxant and pain relievers aggravated her sleep apnea. Up at two a.m. to empty your bladder, you watched with alarm the spasms of her diaphragm. Her lungs failed to draw breath until after you managed to roll her onto her side. She was so tranquilized she slept through the nudging. Where was her CPAP? She explained later that she'd left it behind at Rob's.

"That thing made me feel claustrophobic anyway," she said.

"Apnea is serious business," you said. "It can *kill* you."

But she lacked insurance to pay for a dental device like yours which would keep her tongue from falling into her throat at night. This device might have worked better for Gary's sake, too, since her snoring often awakened him. Despite his reservoirs of patience, you imagined his sleep debt growing and you worried about his health as well.

Not to mention your own. Restful sleep and the solace of dreams eluded you. You grew cranky. Your efforts toward understanding and compassion split like rain-soaked tomatoes on the vine. With aches of your own to manage, you resented Kelley's endless, enervating treks to one hospital after another for more painkillers. They left her with little time and energy for much else. You resented her inability to work and contribute to the household. Especially disheartening was her disengagement, the way she immersed herself in stories she watched onscreen rather than talk with anyone. On 22 May, you tried to update a client's website while yet another movie distracted you in the background—and your frustrations simmered over.

"I'm busting my ass to help support this household," you griped, "and you lounge around all day watching TV like a damn *slug!*"

To your surprise, Kelley jumped up and started throwing things into her bags. "I'm leaving!" she snapped. "I can't deal with you when you're like this!"

The irony of her words stunned you. In peevish silence you let her go as she heroically gathered her belongings and left the house. You both knew there's no bus service this far north on Sundays and she looked too tired to walk very far. Where would she go?

The instinctive urge to hug her farewell seemed awkward and inappropriate so you suppressed it. You forgot your cardinal rule, imposed the day you and your daughter were first separated—the day you began working as a divorced single parent and she began negotiating her way through kindergarten. You resolved then to hug and kiss her whenever you say good-bye, because this could be the last time you see each other. Terrible things happen. Children get kidnapped and parents get mangled in car accidents. You resolved to make sure she knows you love her no matter what. Yet you failed to do that on the Sunday she left your house. In the weeks afterward, you remembered this breach many times.

V. *"We cradled ashes into earth and cicadas began to sing..."* [5]

The end of August, and dahlias and daisies have been blooming fiercely for a month, along with every other flowering plant in Gary's garden. Each day since Kelley's death has brought sunshine and temps in the low 80s. Perfect weather for blossoms and bees. They seem to know the season could end with any sunset. After all, Seattle summers only last a few weeks before the chill and drizzle resume. It's Grand Central Station above the two hives in the backyard, with "the girls" swooping in all directions as they forage for nectar and pollen and water. They remind you of tiny pinballs in their frenzy to build stores for winter.

Questions have ricocheted in your mind every waking minute. What were her last hours like? Nurses and their assistants are often so busy, they're forced to leave patients unattended for many minutes between ministrations. Did she die alone? And who painted her toenails? After all, you found no polish in the baggage she left behind. Did she borrow a bottle from someone on the floor?

You and Gary get copies of her treatment summaries and learn that her doctor had ordered a 24-hour sitter for her. Thank goodness. She needed someone nearby. Solitude only made her anxious. You research sitters and discover they're called PCAs, or personal care assistants, who not only act as caregivers but also as companions when family members are away. It comforts you to imagine shifts of caregiver-companions keeping watch over Kelley during her last five days. Her PCA called the code-blue just after she fell.

After reading the summary, you and Gary accept that the doctors who responded did all they could to save her. But there was simply no response from their patient. The survival rate for CPR is only 18%, not surprising given the violence and invasiveness of the procedure on already weakened patients. But how you wish she had beaten those odds. Time of death was called a minute before midnight yet you prefer to think she was gone as she collapsed at 11:15.

All that potential! And only partially realized. As a gifted child, she dabbled creatively—music, dance, literature, art, drama— and you tried to entice, rather than push her into these interests. Keeping things fun would keep her engaged. She voluntarily took clarinet, piano, trombone, and flute lessons. She studied ballet, marched with her high-school drill team, and earned a Brown Belt in Shotokan Karate. Like you, she enjoyed reading, everything from nonfiction to literature to pulp fiction. Like your mother, she had an eye for perspective and liked to draw and paint. She loved watching movies and her greatest talent may have been acting. She performed in school plays, and later in offices of high-school officials to explain why one of their best students was skipping classes. And later still in courtrooms to petition judicial authorities to give her second and third chances. Her knack for eliciting sympathy often mitigated her punishments.

Did this knack also help destroy her? If only you could have persuaded her to stop! Stop taking all those prescription meds and give her body what it needed to restore balance. Initial cause of death was cardiac failure triggered by pulmonary embolism. Official cause is pending toxicology reports, which could take 8-10 weeks to complete. You could die yourself before then so you gather data to fuel your speculations.

The medical examiner says Kelley's autopsy shows no signs of trauma—the "bruising" was a natural pooling of blood after death—and no pills in her stomach that would indicate suicide. Plus, she was awake when she collapsed, which rules out asphyxiation from apnea as you first thought. Which leads you next to suspect poly-drug interaction. Not an overdose, but a fatal synergy between prescriptions: anti-anxiety med, painkiller, and muscle relaxant. You spend hours researching these tragic interactions, but until those reports confirm specific meds in Kelley's system, you're stymied.

So you put aside the how and ponder the why. Was her death random, or was it predestined? Was her work done here? When she was barely two, your toddler told you something remarkable. She said she slid down the rainbow from heaven into your tummy. "I wanted you for my mommy," she explained, before she had learned about guile. You've forgotten your reply, but no doubt your mind churned: where did she get such an idea? Now, you think maybe her spirit did choose you. Maybe "Kelley's mom" was your calling. Certainly, this role has directed and defined and anchored you for thirty-one years.

If indeed she chose you, did you meet her expectations?

Does that mean your own work here is done? But if you failed, what can you do now? Even if you could arrange at 56 to give birth again, you lack the resources, the monumental stamina, willpower, and time that raising another child would require. Besides, your mother died of heart failure and Alzheimer's disease at 70, and you expect something similar, though sooner than later. Forty years of migraines and a mild stroke last fall put you at risk of full-blown stroke or heart attack which could leave a new child motherless from infancy. No, you cannot initiate such a selfish enterprise even if it means there's a chance Kelley could, or would, choose you again. How can you make it up to her then? Warn the world about fatal poly-drug interactions? Lobby Congress to ban certain medications?

How these ponderings exhaust you! At the heart of it all, you long to believe that Kelley's essence, the laughter and sweetness you treasure from her childhood, is eternal and remains unharmed by human experience.

While organizing her belongings, you remember a CD long tucked away, a disk burned from her Fisher-Price® tape recordings for your birthday ten years ago. You sit and listen anew to the voice of your child singing verses from a song about bumble bees. She must have been five or six and was giggling so much she could barely speak. In the recording, you laugh in the background, just as tickled as she was. Here is unmitigated glee that takes your breath away. Here is undiluted joy as contagious now as it was then. You cannot help but laugh though your tears follow close behind.

When her song is over, she wants you to speak. "Say something weird," she wheedles, "like a joke."

You claim playfully not to know any. "Besides," you say, "my mind's on paying these bills." Your tone slides from silly to somber and immediately she says, "I love you," as if her affection is the most natural and self-evident thing in the world. "I love you too, Kelley," you reply on the CD, your voice brightening, and it's clear that in this archived moment your mind has veered from the mundane to the magical, from the domestic to the divine. You are listening to one soul reveal the unified field theory of life to another. And listening, you remember your last words to each other.

On the night of 22 July, you finally reached her by phone. After you agreed again not to confront Rob (a promise you and Gary now consider breaking), she described what happened since she left your house. The news was upsetting, but the upshot was this: she had left Rob for good—"that son-of-a-bitch, that heartless monster," she said—turning finally to domestic-violence counselors for help. She was shuttling from shelter to shelter for her protection, between Seattle, Tacoma, and Olympia.

"Shelters for battered women," she said, "not for the homeless. Big difference. Private rooms with real furniture for one thing."

You told her you admired her courage. "Thank goodness, you're safe!" you said. "Sweetie, you can stay with us if you need to."

"I'm not a slug."

"I know," you agreed. "Fatigue can make people say things they regret later."

"It's okay, Mom, thanks. But I'll take a raincheck anyway. The house is just too far away. My whole support network is here."

"How about I drive down tomorrow to see you then? Where will you be?"

"I don't know," she said. "They move me day-to-day while they help me look for a safe place to live. I'll call you when I know more." Her nurse arrived to take vital signs and Kelley signed off. "I love you, Mom."

"I love you too, Kelley. Call me soon then, okay? Good night."

You clutch your shoulders now and rock yourself, crying with emotions more intense than ever before: relief, gratitude, anger, anxiety, sorrow. Yet you have faith that you can survive this. *Be thou not afraid...* Here in your sixth decade you're strong enough to travel this path of transitions, despite the heartbreaking work ahead. And the rate of loss can only accelerate with each step: your eyesight, your independence, your memories, your dearest friends. Whenever you falter, you can reach for Kelley's CD to hear her laughter light your way.

And you can hold Gary's first grandchild and giggle as she reads to you someday. You can delight in her joys and help salve her sorrows as she grows. You can spend more time with Jamie, your stepdaughter. Her baby was born the last day in May and already Evelyn's dimpled smile takes your breath away.

VI. *Wallet-Size*

> *Little Miss Watch-Me*
> *with her dandelion smile*
> *dancing on the tips*
> *of her butterfly toes.*
> *She can be thoughtful*
> *once in awhile*
> *but she'd much rather follow*
> *where the soap-bubble blows.*[6]

You read that a child's death is trauma that parents never get over, despite misperceptions to the contrary. Such trauma cannot be overcome and there is no recovery, no return to life as it was. But there *is* integration. Adaptation.[7]

And you can accept this. The work of grief has begun transforming you as water and light transform the seed. With your palms open toward sunlight and rain, you sit each day with the ragged tides of emotion and listen mindfully as they speak about compassion. Not only for Kelley, not only for yourself and Gary, not only for your family and friends, but also for the immense circle of all sentient beings who suffer. This wisdom harvested in the final season of your life shall be your legacy to the teacher and friend who visited you in the guise of your daughter—"a fragrant drop of levity"[8] whose divine spark has returned home to that place where rainbows were born.

"You will heal, and you will rebuild yourself around the loss you have suffered. You will be whole again, but you will never be the same..."[9]

Yet why would you want to be?

In memory of Kelley Marie Smith:
born Saturday afternoon 5 July 1980;
died Saturday night 30 July 2011.

"Good night, sweet rainbow rider, until we meet again..." [10]

Notes:

1. *La Rochefoucauld: Maxims,* trans. Leonard Tancock. Penguin Classics, 1982.
2. Lababidi, Yahia. *Signposts to Elsewhere.* New York: Jane Street Press, 2007.
3. Gibran, Khalil. "On Death," *The Prophet,* trans. Juan R. I. Cole. [http://www-personal.umich.edu/~jrcole/Gibran/prophet/prophet. htm#Death]
4. Gibran, "On Death."
5. Luria-Sukenick, Lynn. "Elegy: Three Months," *The Hue Everyone Living Knows.* Berkley, Parentheses Writing Series, 1993.
6. MacQueen, Donald. "Wallet-Size," written especially for Kelley's sixth birthday. Santa Rosa, California, 1986.
7. Bernstein, Judith R., Ph.D. *When the Bough Breaks.* Kansas City: Andrews McMeel Publishing, LLC, 1998.
8. *Basic Writings of Nietzsche,* trans. Walter Kaufman. New York: Random House Publishing, Modern Library, 2000.
9. Kübler-Ross, Elizabeth and David Kessler. *On Grief and Grieving.* New York: Scribner, 2007.
10. Brenna, Duff. Personal quotation for Kelley's eulogy, 2011. Duff's novels, especially *The Book of Mamie* and *The Altar of the Body,* were among her favorites.

Bette Lynch Husted

Morning at the Western Gate Health Club

I'm free,
free fallin'

We belt it out off-key, Cassie
turning up her iPod, flashing us that smile—
she thinks it's sweet we like the older tunes—
"Increased resistance," she calls. "Standing Hill!"
Bent low over the handlebars, I wonder
where Tom Petty is these days—still
Going to the End of the Line?

sometimes you gotta be strong
we're breathing hard
free fallin'
young Tom's leaving
a good girl, crazy 'bout Elvis,
loves horses and her boyfriend too—
but there are other ways to fall

like the way I track the symptoms
of your illness
as if I could follow close enough
to close the gap   catch you in my arms—

both of us old enough to know
loving and leaving are always
the same thing—

"Fast and easy, race pace!"
Sweating now, we pedal down the other side
with Credence, *it ain't me*
I ain't no fortunate one
though of course I am
feeling for purchase
spinning away

Alicia Ostriker

Insomnia

But it's really fear you want to talk about
and cannot find the words
so you jeer at yourself

you call yourself a coward
you wake at 2 a.m. thinking failure,
fool, unable to sleep, unable to sleep

buzzing away on your mattress with two pillows
and a quilt, they call them comforters,
which implies that comfort can be bought

and paid for, to help with the fear, the failure
your two walnut chests of drawers snicker, the bookshelves mourn
the art on the walls pities you, the man himself beside you

asleep smelling like mushrooms and moss is a comfort
but never enough, never, the ceiling fixture lightless
velvet drapes hiding the window

traffic noises like a vicious animal

on the loose somewhere out there—
you brag to friends you won't mind death only dying

what a liar you are—
all the other fears, of rejection, of physical pain,
of losing your mind, of losing your eyes,

they are all part of this!
Pawprints of this! Hair snarls in your comb—
Now notice the clock is the single light in the room—

Leslie What

Three Sisters Have We in Our House

Chance made us sisters, hearts made us friends.
—Author Unknown

I am the middle of three sisters. As children we were a tightly braided group who stood united against a repressive regime, AKA Mom and Dad. Our braid loosened as we became teenagers, unraveled into three separate strands once we escaped the family home to establish our own households. My little sister, Stephanie, stayed closest to the SoCal family homestead. My big sister, Carolyn, moved to the Bay area. I moved 1,000 miles to the north to get away from my parents, but that move had the unintended effect of keeping me away from my sisters.

Carolyn was the first to realize we siblings were squandering a treasure. To solve the problem, she arranged a sisters-only getaway in Las Vegas. At first we felt guilty for not inviting our husbands or our mom. The guilt vanished after the second round of drinks at the hotel. One weekend of desert debauchery was enough to rekindle our sisterly love and since then, we have treated each other as treasured friends, making an effort to see one another several times a year.

Each sister is involved in, as they say in the personal ads, Long Term Relationships (LTR). We have loved our husbands since we were young women and we expect to grow old alongside them. If you added up the years we've been with our partners, they would top one hundred. Yet the LTR between the sisters extends even further, and during one of our sisters' weekends, we fell into a frank discussion about what it meant to age. We came up with the radical notion that the three of us would live together after our husbands were dead.

This might sound heartless but we were just being practical. Though the margin has narrowed from 7.9 to 5 years since 1979, on average women live longer than men. Both my father and my father-in-law died a decade or more before their wives. My sisters watched the pattern repeat with their in-laws. It is a fact of life that more women outlive their husbands than the other way around.

My husband is six years older than I am. According to the CDC, I will outlive him by five years. On the statistical graph that is our lives, my column will rise above his by eleven years. If I had my druthers, I'd go first. It was my task to deal with childbirth and in a just world, my husband would face the ugly task of negotiating with a funeral director whose livelihood depends upon the ever-escalating cost of guilt (as measured by the ever-escalating price of a casket).

A few more sobering statistics: If you're an old woman, you have a greater chance of living in a nursing home at the end of your life than does a man (three quarters of nursing home residents are women). Twice as many women over 75 are poor compared to elderly men (13% compared to 6%). Our mother, may her memory bring a blessing, raised us to believe that there had to be pluses whenever there were minuses. My sisters and I thought we'd found *the plus* in our plan to live together when we were old.

I wanted to talk to my sweetie about this, but never got up the nerve to ask, "Got any plans for when I'm dead?" Until one evening, halfway through a glass of wine a bartender had poured like he was drafting a pint, when I blurted out our sisterly scheme. My spouse of thirty years looked off into the distance with an absentminded smile of someone thumbing through a catalogue who doesn't really want to buy anything, but isn't quite ready to recycle the paper. I let the subject drop for another few months.

The truth is, we're not quite old enough to seriously worry about dying. I have at least another fifteen years before, if I die suddenly, people older than me will stop saying, "But she was so young!" We haven't even finished making our wills. The discussion about the three sisters living together seemed so let's-pretend-and-far -away that we didn't speak of it again.

Then my sister Carolyn bought the house.

She found a remodeled Craftsman home on a tree-lined street an hour away from San Francisco, with three bedrooms and two bathrooms on the first floor, and a fenced yard. Our theoretical house now had a roof and a dog run and was centrally located. Stephanie was the first to visit, and during that visit she claimed the back corner bedroom for herself. My room is in the middle, just across the hall from the bathroom. It overlooks the backyard garden and is a perfectly lovely room, though of course I worry that Stephanie's might be nicer. Sibling rivalry doesn't end when you grow up.

My husband admits a tinge of jealousy for our planned home for aged sisters, but he is also relieved to know I won't be on my own. He saw his mother's loneliness, saw how she never fully recovered from her husband's death. Lil met Danny while both served in the armed forces during WWII and they stayed together more than fifty years. In her twenties, Lil had been a brave and adventurous soul who had joined the Army Nurse Corps and worked in the Pacific Theater, but as a widow in her seventies, the time for grand adventure had passed. She was waiting, she often said, to join her soul mate in heaven. After Danny's death, she still poured twelve cups of water into her percolator and threw away what she didn't drink at the end of the day. She saw no point in learning to make a single cup of coffee.

My mother was widowed while in her fifties, young enough to give her time for her adventures to begin again. After my father's lethargic old Schnauzer died (a dog that looked and acted like a log on four legs), my mother chose her own canine BFF (best friend forever), and for the first time in her life, she picked a pet's name without the interference and direction of her spouse or her children. Acknowledging the nature of their relationship, she named him, "Shadow." It may seem insignificant, but choosing the dog's name is an autonomous declaration many women don't experience until after their children are gone and their husbands are dead. Allowing someone else to name the dog she will most likely be stuck feeding and cleaning up after is another small nick in the timeline of small sacrifices women make to keep the peace.

My mother stayed in the house she had shared with my father for another ten years, until she grew lonely living alone in a neighborhood of happy couples and young families. She was getting older and she recognized that it was time to move. She instructed her adult children to come get those childhood belongings we had left with her for semi-permanent safekeeping, those things we had not wanted to take with us once we left home, but had not been ready to discard. Unlike us, she was ready to abandon hastily crafted plaster handprints and middle school badges earned for excellence in housekeeping and French, her ghastly collection of ceramic ashtrays we'd made in school as Mother's Day gifts. The reality of downsizing always trumps any desire to hold onto someone else's past, and our mother boxed up her house and moved to a gated retirement community called The Colony, where most of her neighbors were active single women in their sixties.

She flourished in the company of women and soon formed close friendships. She learned to play cards and Mah Jongg and use a computer (she had never learned to type). She was friendly with her neighbors, but when one neighbor died suddenly from a heart attack, my mother became a mentor to the grieving widow, teaching her all she'd learned about going on instead of thinking your life was over.

Unlike my mother, Lil grieved every day. She'd become a widow in her late seventies, an age that was less welcoming to radical lifestyle changes. She was able to live independently until her eyesight and health deteriorated to the point that she conceded it was time to move in with her daughter. When her daughter's multiple sclerosis flared, my mother-in-law packed up her big screen TV and heavy raincoat and moved in with my husband and me, during my last year of graduate school and a term when I was teaching two classes and commuting three hours each way. I'd only recently been diagnosed with Crohn's disease, a chronic autoimmune disorder. I chugged Prednisone by the bucket and felt so sick I nearly took a leave of absence from school. It was an inconvenient time, from my perspective.

Lil struggled to thrive in a home she did not own, with unfamiliar foods and without friends to help her sneak cigarettes, and without the ability to navigate outside the house on her own. She was always thankful and gracious about my cooking, respectful of my writing. Her mother had been a poet, she said, but all her poems were destroyed or lost after her death, and Lil could not remember any of them.

We muddled through the stress as best we could, even became close friends. One of Lil's favorite proverbs was a line from an Isaac Watts poem, "Birds in their little nests must agree." We mostly managed not to push the other birds from our little nest, even when we felt like shoving them off the tree.

Though Lil could not remember her mother's poetry she had memorized many poems and she quoted Whitman's "O Captain! My Captain!" from memory. She grasped the concept of the Internet from my explanation, even though her macular degeneration kept her from using, or even seeing a keyboard. Getting to know her was a blessing. But we never learned how to talk to one another about the difficulties of our situation.

We thought a puppy would be a welcome distraction, and with me in the back seat, my husband drove us out to the country where we found a friendly and energetic spotted terrier. It was love at first touch. Lil fussed over that puppy and swaddled her in a blanket and held the puppy in the tight hold of a nurse trained to prevent nursery uprisings. "I think there would be world peace," she said, "if every leader got to hold a puppy in his arms." She freed the puppy from the crate I had purchased to potty train the dog, and hid the cleanup efforts from me, rarely successfully. We locked into a territorial conflict about what to name the puppy. Lil wanted to call her Missy. I wanted to call her Stella.

My husband did not understand why it meant so much to dig in my heels and keep dog-naming rights to myself, why I was so angry with Lil for calling the dog Missy whenever I was out of the room. He found himself in the unfortunate position of being a referee for the fight between mother and wife. Before the fight could escalate further, Lil reconsidered. She agreed to call the dog Stella.

Oh, the guilt. It wasn't yet my time to name a dog. In my selfishness I had denied Lil a rare chance to name a pet. Perhaps that's one reason she left our home after eight months and returned to live with her daughter, where she stayed until illness overwhelmed her and she was placed in a care facility for a few months before her death.

Now and then I'll sing the refrain of Michael Bolton's "How Can I Live Without You" to reassure my spouse that I will miss him terribly when he's gone. And I will miss him, even with a puppy to console me. After thirty years you know your partner well enough to be together in silence. But it is never really quiet. There's always the background noise of another person, the sniffle and fabric rustle and the turning of the newspaper page or tapping of the keyboard to remind you that you are not alone.

A 2005 survey commissioned by Johnson & Johnson found that 56% of all caregivers are women and more than half are over the age of forty-five. In the past, it took a village to care for the elders, but as village life evolved and extended families went nuclear, women have assumed the burden of caring for the elderly.

After my mother had trouble breathing in 2008, her doctor ordered an X-ray, which showed a shadow. I flew down and met my sisters and our mom for her bronchoscopy appointment. Together we learned that my mother had lung cancer and her prognosis was terminal. Most people in her condition died within six months. There was no treatment and she should never again be left alone. In one day, all of our lives changed. If our mother could not be left alone, who was to stay with her?

Because my work as a writer had the most flexible schedule, and because I had trained as a nurse, I became the primary caregiver. Stephanie stayed Friday night to Sunday. Carolyn traveled frequently for work, but between trips, she stayed at our mother's. It was expensive and inconvenient for me to fly home for less than four days at a time, so to get away I sometimes stayed overnight in a nearby motel. I may have been the primary caregiver, but for eight months, none of the three sisters took time off from our mother's cancer.

Our mother, like many mothers, was a wonderful woman, but a difficult patient. She had grown up in Germany in an extended and loving family, with younger siblings and parents and elderly aunts, all of whom were murdered by the Nazis after the family was deported to the Riga Ghetto in 1941. My mother was orphaned as a young woman, spared only because she was strong enough to work as a slave laborer. She learned never to trust anyone and to hide all signs of weakness. If someone was too weak to work, they were put to death. My mother was terrified of showing her vulnerability. The very skills that had helped her to survive the Holocaust worked against her when confronting a terminal disease. She told her doctor that her pain was manageable then complained bitterly when she was alone with us.

My mother had become a bit of a pack rat. When residents in The Colony died, restrictive covenants forbade their heirs from holding estate sales on the property. Neighbors were invited to pick through the things that might otherwise have been sold for a quarter. My mother frequented these giveaways. Her garage cabinets were filled with wasp spray and fertilizer and paint thinner and knickknacks. The garage walls were atherosclerotic with boxes of wrapping paper gleaned from the garages of the dead. She had at least ten of every tool ever forged to prune branches. She surrounded herself with stuff, a reaction, I think, to that time when everything had been taken from her. She was used to living in the space of her home, but now that she needed a caregiver and a walker, it became impossible to navigate through the garage. The sisters tried to clear some space, taking a few pesticides to the dump, returning plastic water bottles for redemption. But our mother fought every attempt to recycle or toss. We were taking away all that was important to her. She screamed at me when she caught me about to recycle a cardboard box from a kitchen faucet she'd had installed many years before. "It's got a lifetime guarantee!" she yelled, and I did not argue.

She always had at least twenty-five pounds of butter in the freezer and perhaps fifty pounds of flour sealed in four-gallon Tupperware canisters. When Albertsons had a sale on sugar, she instructed me to buy four bags and to pick up another six pounds of butter because she wanted to be sure to have enough for her Christmas baking.

As a nurse, I had sat with dozens of people as they took their last breaths, but my mother's experiences with death were vastly more unsettling. I had been at my mother-in-law's bedside the moment her breathing changed, and I ran to call in the family from another room (where they were meeting with a counselor) so they could be with her as she took her final breaths. Her children and grandchildren stood around Lil's bed, holding hands, singing, wishing her an easy passing. Death ends the struggle and pain that can define the end of life, and watching Lil die taught us what it means to be at rest. My mother raged, raged against the dying of the light. To her, death was seeing families shoved into cattle cars, children pulled from their mothers, her family taken away in gas vans. She did not want to tell anyone, not her friends, not her neighbors, not her rabbi about her illness. We sisters understood her terror, her fear, her rage.

She alternately praised me for cooking and told me that my meals reminded her of the terrible foods at the camps. She woke up screaming for her Mutti. "Don't let them take me away," she screamed in the middle of her nightly nightmares. She asked us to sleep with her in her bed. She held our hands and planted kisses on the lips, openly affectionate in ways she had never before shared. My husband says that mothers and daughters compete with one another in ways that sons and mothers never see. Sometimes my mother's frustration pushed her natural critical tendencies. Sometimes she was surprisingly mean. One evening she deliberately ran into me with her walker, wanting to hurt me because I had locked the door to keep her from going out at night. Another time she bragged that she was thin and gave me a withering glance and said that she did not want to get fat, like me. She accused me of trying to kill both her and her dog with pain pills. She said other mean things to my sisters, but the three of us understood that cancer and medication were overwhelming her sensibilities. And there were other days, days when she wrote us notes to thank us for sticking with her. She tested us and pushed, pushed, pushed us away, but we never abandoned her.

My mother kept the television on at night because she was afraid of the quiet. The noise made it difficult to sleep. Lack of sleep and stress are accelerants that fuel auto-immune disorders like Crohn's, and I was ill much of the time, though my illness, like most of the problems of my life, paled by comparison to my mother's.

Caring for her grew increasingly difficult. She was belligerent.

She refused to take her pain and anxiety pills. She was withdrawn when close friends visited. From the start her wish had been to stay in her home, but reluctantly, the sisters discussed sending her to a nursing home, and we scouted out those that were near. They smelled bad and the residents looked dirty. The rooms looked like barracks. We knew our mother would be humiliated and terrified to be taken down the hall wrapped in a robe to the communal showers. We could not do it. Finally, she agreed to be seen by hospice and we had someone to call for help in managing her pain and terror.

Carolyn came across an endearing expression in a novel by Lisa See: "laotong," which literally means "old same" but describes the lifelong (and beyond) relationships between women bound as kindred sisters. During our mother's illness we began referring to each other as precious laotongs. We wrote each other notes, confessing high and low points and sharing details of the day. "Dearest laotongs" all of our emails began.

Two weeks before my mother died, on a night when she was especially agitated and unable to sit still or eat, she asked me to chant the Shema, a statement of deep faith that traditional Jews are told to say as their last prayers. We had never been an observant family, but I had learned a bit about Judaism after having children, and I knew this prayer and understood its significance. I taught her the words and helped her chant it and that calmed her a bit. I asked her then what she wanted us to do when she died. She did not want to talk about it, but it felt like a now or never moment, and I pushed a little harder than was comfortable. She told me she wished to have the traditional Jewish washing ritual of Tahara performed after her death. She told me who to call and what to say. She told me she didn't care what we did with her as long as we did not bury her beside my father.

My husband once told me that women have friends but men just have their wives. It's good that women build social networks into their lives, he said, because it allows us to adapt to surviving the loss of a spouse in ways that men cannot. Living longer is a blessing and a curse. Sure, we have a few more years but those years provide more time to bury the people we love. A longer life is a bit of an ironic insult to women, who see more than our fair share of inequity and grief.

When my mother died, my husband sat in another room and read aloud the prescribed prayers meant to purify her soul while I bathed her spirit and body as best as I could do according to Jewish tradition. I dressed her in white linens provided by the Jewish Burial Society in Oregon. Stephanie made arrangements with the funeral home, and Carolyn saw to financial matters. Fatigue took over. We sank into the shadows of sadness that still darken some days nearly three years later.

It's true that no matter how many people stand at the bedside, each person dies alone. It's also true that those who live on afterwards need a village. We three sisters first lived in that village when we were children. We returned there to help our mother live and help her die. We will visit that village once again when we are old.

It took almost ten months after our mother died to sort through her belongings and ready the home for sale. We kept what we could keep and gave many of her things to her dearest friends. We used Freecycle and Craigslist for the small things and rented a dumpster for what we could not give away. We found someone to take the freezer and most of its contents. Carolyn took home the vats of flour, an ice chest filled with butter, the pounds of sugar.

A few weeks ago her husband saw the flour canisters in a closet and questioned who in the world could ever need so much? When Carolyn told me this, I laughed. I told Stephanie, and she laughed, too. We weren't laughing at him for asking a perfectly reasonable question. We were laughing at ourselves for understanding everything without needing to ask why.

Husbands come and go; children come and eventually they go. Friends grow up and move away. But the one thing that's never lost is your sister.
　　　　　　　　　　　　—Gail Sheehy

Elisabeth Murawski

Incense for the Blithe

She has been searching forever
for the icehouse where God's supposed to live
and here she is in the tropics,

in the midst of orchids (it kills her
to die in the midst of orchids)
with a snowy egret feather in her hair.

She wants nothing more than the sun
and the sun wants to set fire to everything.
Objects she once made space for

go up in quintessential smoke.
The power's off. The room is dark.
She practices push-ups

on the difficult road to the angels.
Every birth counts she says aloud
touching her chin to the floor.

The corners of her mouth soften.
A light swims out from her head
to play on the glistening planet.

She releases a family of finches,
on the advice of Socrates
burns incense for the blithe.

Leigh Anne Jasheway

If It's Good Enough for the Coffee Table . . .

The other day, I was in the bathroom applying alpha-beta-kappa-delta hydroxy acid to my crows' feet in a feeble attempt to look like my twenty-something self. Okay, my early thirty-something self. All right, I'd have settled for the way I looked three days earlier.

As I went about my daily routine in the bathroom, I could hear the television in the living room. This is because my house is so small that I can dust the entire thing while keeping one foot planted in the hall. So I could plainly hear every word the chatty host had to say.

At one point, just as I was wondering whether it wouldn't be cheaper to just reapply the oil from my forehead onto my cheeks and save several hundred dollars a year, I heard something coming from the TV that demanded my attention. It was the following statement: "The distressed look is really trendy today."

I immediately dropped my $47 bottle of moisturizer into the sink and ran into the living room, hoping to see women half my age squinting and scowling in order to add a few wrinkle lines in pursuit of this new hot new trend. What I saw instead was, of course, a home decorating show. The host was "distressing" a piece of new furniture so that it looked worn and lived with. The same look I had been trying to erase from my face.

Why is it that we want our furniture to look aged and

ourselves to look youthed? (Somebody was going to make this word up sooner or later and it might as well be me.) I keep waiting for articles to appear on the front cover of *Seventeen Magazine* with headlines such as "Smile Today—Pay Later" or "Ten Ways to Keep From Ever Moving Your Eyebrows." Let's face it; if we're going to stop these nasty, face-aging habits, we have to start young.

It's just part of the American Dream: Life, liberty, and the pursuit of making things into something they aren't. If it's old, we want it to look new. If it's curly, we want it straight. If it's fat, we want it to be thin, or at least guilty. Fixing things that aren't broke is our national pastime.

As I stood there watching the TV decorator beating a table with a chain and then scratching it with steel wool so that it could have the look I had attained naturally, I decided I'd had enough. I switched off the tube, walked back into the bathroom and proceeded to throw tubes and jars and bottles into the trash can. Out went the anti-oxidant creams, the elasticin eye-firming gel (which I will admit I once tried on my chest, but the results were inconclusive) and the wrinkle defense system. ("General, the wrinkles are gaining on us! Shall we bring in the big guns?") Of course, I saved the moisturizer with SPF and all my make-up. After all, I was fed up, not crazy.

Then I looked at myself in the bathroom mirror. Sure, I looked a little like a Sharpei. But you know what? If it's good enough for my coffee table, it's good enough.

Bette Lynch Husted

Blowback

*Blowback: the backpressure in an internal combustion
engine, or the powder residue that is released upon
automatic ejection of a spent cartridge or shell from
a firearm. Also a metaphor used by the CIA for
the unintended negative consequences of the US
government's international activities.*

Mothers hugged us. Fathers bought ice cream, held out
paint by number promises; elders whispered
prayers to ward off hunger, Depression, A-bombs.
Antibiotics

blessed our colds. When Holocaust photos showed us
more than we could bear, we knew things were changing.
Rosa Parks said No. Martin Luther King had
been to the mountain.

Our war caught us unprepared. Priests in prison,
monks on fire, that little girl running, burning.
We were no one's fortunate sons. Friends died by
lottery. Some chose

exile, some returned to us broken. Tear gas,
Agent Orange, white phosphorus. Tet Offensive,

Green Berets, the Pentagon Papers, My Lai
Massacre. Leeches.

Now we sit in airports with soldiers wearing
desert camo, boys leaving mothers younger
than ourselves. One woman is trying not to
touch her son, though she

reaches toward his neck before she remembers.
In the corner President Bush explains why
this war must go on. No one listens. This boy
stiffens to silence—

head shaved, slender, boots lacing toward his knees like
earth-clad bones. We think of our own sons, of their
eyes. Imagination has failed us. Now he's
waved off his family

turned to face the runway ahead. His younger
brothers tip their heads back to scan the sky for
one last look, the plane lifting off and blowback
shaping their future.

Photo by Todd Cooper

Diane McWhorter

Stay Calm, Nothing Is Under Control

Rain or shine, I stand in company at the *Eugene Saturday Market* surrounded by what I have created. Of the seventeen booths in my neighborhood on the downtown Park Blocks, six of them hold the work of women in their sixties or seventies. Teresa, on the corner near Oak Street, has sold here the longest, crafting wind chimes from silverware. She brings her grandchildren to help. Levana lines her booth with tie-dye t-shirts, from tiny to triple-extra-large, including transformed tightie-whities. Romantic illustrations glow in Nancy Bright's booth, reproduced in cards and journals, even bookmarks for a dollar. Cheryl and David make metal-worked jewelry together, but she does the selling. He made a canopy for their booth of felted orange and white koi, creating an underwater garden above.

I'm around the corner from their row, my booth open on the sides for visibility, shaded by two big green umbrellas and backed up to the big fountain. My printed baseball caps perch on twigs of an apple branch zip-tied to my portable rack. Folding shelves hold neat stacks of t-shirts, and I have six kinds of nature-themed canvas tote bags on the outside of one wall. Five men from my generation sit in their booths on the other side of the aisle, including Willy, who sells drums with Native-American inspired designs and t-shirts, and serves as the Market Board President. Next to me, in his corner spot, Raven entertains all with his rattles and shakers—sculpted with the faces of fanciful, friendly creatures—made from sawdust and cellulose and embellished with crystals and feathers. Bill makes Italian-inspired mosaics on picture frames, mirrors, and guitars; Gil brings more paintings now than candles, and he and Gary, who makes ceramics, have held down that corner with Teresa for as long as anyone can remember.

At ten, when the Market opens, Raven leads a tiny parade around the block, welcoming us with rhythm and a song: *"Saturday, Saturday, Saturday Market. Prosperity and fun for everyone. The magic has begun for everyone. . . ."* The sparse singers are often off-key, but we all sing along and appreciate the reminder of what brings us here. More than our source of income, Saturday is our social day, our chance to shop, and our weekly spiritual commune with family and friends.

It's a tough, twelve-hour day, with over two hours of set-up and take-down time at the start and finish, but I've been practicing this for thirty-six years. I have an easy, grandmotherly appearance that works for me and products that appeal to a wide range of customers. I practice familiar rituals: hanging back in the corner by my chair with a helpful look as browsers get close to decisions, staying alert and attentive to their needs. People seem to appreciate the way I express my sense of humor with baseball hats that say "Geezer Gone Wild" and "I make stuff up," and t-shirts printed with "Stay calm, nothing is under control." I use my stock lines often. "Older than dirt" brings the response ". . . and twice as good looking!" Whether the public decides to purchase or pass, I'm here to present, not to win. And I'm definitely not here just to make money.

My community is an artisan community. We are the *older* craftspeople: stubborn remnants of a 60s subculture, leftover hippies of the Peace and Love Revolution movement, hard workers who use our art forms to generate income. In 1970, we cooperatively created space for more than two hundred artisans. Our weekly market has thrived ever since, responding with "high touch" to an increasingly

143

"high tech" world. There is a management team of mature women who work to enhance our sales by discovering and implementing efficient and practical solutions to our challenges. Emphasis is placed on equality and non-competitive, mutual support. I help Raven put up his pop-up canopy, and he brings me an oatmeal scone from the New Day Bakery. Everybody offers advice to a young strolling vendor, and I trade him a Jell-O Art slug for a pair of his origami earrings. Willy and I collaborate on some of his products, and we're close friends even though we both sell t-shirts.

Each vendor's art is personal, and we laugh at the term "unique." We're beyond labels; we have generated original lives and jobs for ourselves. We're cooks and musicians and jewelers; we sew and dye; we build furniture, shoes, and sculptures. Often we sell several things at once: cheesecake and pine needle baskets, knitted scarves and felted toys, stamped metal pet tags on one counter and gourmet donuts on the other. Curious and engaged with art in many forms, we've all experimented widely over the decades. My house is full of products—my own and those of other Market artisans—that at first contained hope but now sit dusty with discouragement. It's a rich life, but most of us earn incomes well below the poverty level. Quality of life choices—value choices—were made long ago: independence and control of time trumped making loads of money.

Creating beauty and fun is my response to a world I can't control, a way to keep myself centered and to find and communicate who I am. The constant feedback amidst music and flowers—the discovery and joy shared with people who understand me—sustains me and guides what I choose to make. I wouldn't thrive without my Market. We've grown up together.

My Market is the most gentle business network imaginable. Each member gets a temporary 8 x 8 foot square of real estate in the center of town, across the street from the heirloom tomatoes and hybrid sweet corn of the Farmers' Market. Every artisan pays a flat fee of ten dollars, plus ten percent of what he or she earns—on the honor system. We sell only what we make, grow, or transform, and standards are strictly monitored by a large volunteer committee. Our business incubator has generated hundreds of successful local enterprises. Many sellers come and go: some to bigger ventures, some without developing the mix of skills needed to progress beyond the making of things into the intuitive areas of customer and self-satisfaction. It's a subtle art in itself, but everything hinges on it.

If I'm lucky and manage my transactions with finesse, a husband might pick out a hat while his wife chooses a tote bag or a shirt for a grandchild. Everything matters: my coffee breath, my scowl at the weather, or my flat joke may convince them they don't need to make a purchase right this minute. I hide my need and just show my delight. I put my effort into my crafts and display and attempt to intuit the hidden needs of strangers. If they do decide to buy, they hand me the item, and then the money, and I hand back the change from the organized wallet I wear around my waist. I ask about a bag, and if I feel particularly good about the way our interaction went, I might give them a locally-made canvas bag I've printed with the Market logo. It has a retail price of five dollars, so they are pleased to feel that special. I want them to come back, feel richer for their spending; I want them to understand a little more of what brings me here. I don't do it just for myself but for the survival of my community.

An admirer wants to get close to what I make, but she doesn't really need any of my products. She's curious about my possibilities, my artistic edge, and my risk, but views it from a safe distance. She wants to touch what I am, in a way that feels comfortable and generous to both of us, and she can't know how exposed and vulnerable I feel. If all goes well she will leave my booth with a piece of what I do, and I will get to pay my bills and come back the following week. Of course, I'll come back even if the transaction doesn't go well. Persistence pays off.

During the selling day, I don't think too much about this

complicated dance, just try for flexibility and grace. Long ago, I learned to stuff down the constant fear of insolvency and ill health, and trust the flow of money and good luck. My sturdy constitution is built on superstition and wishful thinking, applied with dogged practicality. With every new design, I fall into the same trap of joyous expectation and the subsequent adjustment to reality when my new products fail to excite ownership. I will bring things for months if people like them, even if they don't really sell, adjusting prices, position, and presentation. My booth is always a work in progress.

On a sunny day, when the aisles are packed and the tally on my clipboard is filling up the page, I think I might be doing this right. But when it doesn't seem to be my day, I fight off the doubt. I made it through years of overwork, growing the business well enough to buy houses and raise children. In my fifties, I peaked with professional success and am now in the transition to the end of it all. Each Saturday brings a new opportunity to fly or fail, each new trend a choice to follow or find myself left behind. Every week I come to this home place by the fountain, soft and hungry, strong and determined, grateful but diminished.

The physical demands of my day outside are huge. I bring my whole setup to Market on a big bike cart, much as I did in the late seventies when I built a booth out of 2 x 2s that converted to a cart. That first one didn't last, but the ease of hauling a cart-load right to my booth space, bypassing the need for a fossil-fueled truck and a lot of shuffling, keeps me in the tiny group of a dozen human-powered vendors. I'm on my fourth cart now, a utility trailer called a "Hauler," locally custom-built at the Center for Appropriate Transport.

My trailer has a special hitch to my bike-seat post that cost $100 alone. The diamond-plate aluminum bed is 3' x 4', and it can carry a quarter-ton bungeed to its low rails of powder-coated chromoly steel tubing. With my shoulder-high piles of plastic tubs, baskets, and fixtures, topped off with the rustic hat rack, I look like a particularly clean and organized bag lady.

The last time I weighed my load it was 534 pounds, not including the bike, trailer, and me. When it's balanced right, with the weight forward and over the wheels, the load rolls comfortably down the street powered by my strong, lean cyclist's legs. Whenever I start and stop, I feel the value of momentum, and a curb cut is the toughest hill I can attempt. I've worked to lessen the load, but a lot of it is essential. If I slip and break a bone, or rupture another disk, my transition will become a trial. I'll need to use my old car, get friends to help, and at some point move to the small 4' x 4' spaces on the perimeter as I lose the points necessary to sell in the center. I joke that I will die on the Park Blocks, and it could be a comparatively pleasant way to go, watching the sun filter through the cedar trees one last time.

It's not really funny. I can't retire. I do need the cardio workout that is the thirty-minute ride from my house, but when I bike, the way I jut my head forward makes my arms fall asleep. I don't stick to my lifting limit of twenty-five pounds. I bring too much. My survival in this particular style of outdoor selling is as tenuous and unpredictable as the weather. Autumn comes with darkness when I rise and when I trundle home, and the rainy days can be dangerous and draining. Even a small load is a traffic hazard on the wrong street at the wrong time. One morning the cart was badly loaded and tipped back, dangling the bike in the air, and my 130 pounds wasn't enough to bring it down. I had to unload and start over and was almost too late to claim my space.

While it's my job to find a way to bring my goods to the marketplace, I depend on my membership organization to deliver the customers. A high priority is placed on member and customer amenities that provide the public a safe place to explore. Management maintains the conditions of the public workplace, including security workers and people to clean the tables in the food court and pick up the garbage. They keep the structure functional and make it easy to enter so we have a constantly renewing group of craftsmen and women to serve the enthusiastic tourists and locals.

The Market supports our struggle to stay current by protecting tradition while moving with the times. Many of us blog and Facebook and have websites for online marketing, assisted by our Promotions Manager in her seminars. Instant transactions are often handled by smart phones. The younger craftspeople and customers set the conditions now, but together we all navigate the mainstream. We carry forward the ancient tradition of cottage industry, presented for exchange in the public gathering place. The big things don't change, just the details.

Most of us have inadequate retirement plans, savings, or safety nets. Health insurance, if we even have it, is catastrophic. Our management is often called upon to assist one of us in some aspect of the death process, with a grant from the member emergency fund, to spread the word that someone needs help, or to place a vase of flowers and a card on an empty booth space after someone passes. This year's been especially rough, losing community members every month. Our founder, Lotte Streisinger, still comes to shop although her days as a potter are over, and she pushes a walker now instead of a cart. The treasures our elders bring us can never be replaced, but they live on in story and the skills they shared. Some old ones take on apprentices or pass on their craft skills to offspring, but for the most part, our art, carrying the marks of our hands, is what keeps our sparks burning just a little bit longer than our own breath.

Each evening as I wrestle my cart into my shed, I know I won't be able to do this as long as I will need to. I must develop a craft that is lightweight, that doesn't require an investment in inventory, one that doesn't need to be screen-printed. Something practical and useful would be best, but I have that part covered if I can still print the hats and the canvas tote bags. I'll have to abandon the shirt printing that is my source of outside-the-Market income. I've given myself five years to explore new products, to expand my artistry into the fringes of what I can master, and to leave behind the production work I can no longer physically manage.

I may have stumbled upon my answer to the future with my "Jell-O Art," my newest product, one that astonishes people and stops them in their tracks. The orchids, roses, and fascinators I make with dried gelatin are creating a buzz. I call it Gelatinaceae, a new botanical family, and it is a riot of turquoise, fuchsia, and golden yellow in my formerly cool-colored display of moss green and black.

It's not new to me; I've been a Jell-O artist for twenty-three years. We have an annual April Fools show at a local gallery. The dried gelatin I make in thin layers is not jiggly but glass-like in its brilliant transparency. I glue the pieces together with the molten gelatin. People are intrigued and touched by the seductive beauty of the flowers and personality of the gelatin creatures. It's more ephemeral than glass, and may never be fine art, but the joy it brings to my tiny spot on the planet is well worth the experiment.

The true passion the pieces communicate hits people in the center of their unspoken needs. It's a kitchen art that anyone can do. I tell all my secrets on my blog, but nobody can make it like I make it. Gelatin, water, dye, time, plus the artist's eye; it's very simple. I get a new set of stock responses: "Can you eat it?" "Only if you're desperate."

I shake the little jar of colorless, sugarless powder that is the source of all that loveliness, the source that has allowed me to express myself more precisely than any other art form; my life summed up in a light, gorgeous, vibrant green and purple useless object. I stand as high as I ever have, with my offering to the goddesses of art, in humility and gratitude.

Just enough of it has sold this season to keep me interested. If my transition to the future can be this colorful, this easy, this thrilling, I don't need to worry. The cart, the fixtures, and the structures can all be adapted, and I clearly can be, too. I've struck a chord. Now I just have to keep dancing, with a Jell-O Art orchid in my thinking grey hair, as the music plays on the corner of 8th and Oak.

This past weekend, I took my turn in our ritualistic Saturday morning parade. Raven pranced, Sheila jingled her finger cymbals as she twirled, and Willy's drumbeat was strong and even. We felt our power. After a warm group hug, we all got back to work, light and full in the summer sun, happy to receive what the Market would bring this day, happy to have something to give.

Jan Eliot

Gravity

R.A. Rycraft

Ten Ways to Look at Boob Jobs

The breasts I knew at midnight beat like the sea in me now.
—Anne Sexton

ONE: The basic Boob Job is not necessarily a matter of choice. Take my own, for instance.

I never wanted one. But menopause hit with its extra twenty pounds (and counting), and I have a free Boob Job. I'd say nature has *out-jugged* itself when it comes to my bust—not to mention the rest of me. Turned my 34Cs into 38Ds. I stand in front of the mirror and check out my bare breasts. I tell myself, They don't look so bad. Your fifty-five-year-old puppies look pretty good, especially when you factor in the four kids they've survived. Pendulous, maybe, but not bovine.

I turn this way and that, cup them in my hands, push them together, evaluate the cleavage and am shocked to realize that no push-up bra is going to help. Clearly, gravity and two pounds of connective tissue, ligaments, milk-glands, fibroid cysts, and fat are sufficient to push them over the edge. The weight of them sagging into bra-cups, Judi Dench-like, rather than spilling out of them, Helen Mirren-like. That blue corset I wore as a "treat" for my honey before his research trip to the Yukon nine years ago? History. The black leather one I wore for our eighth anniversary? Hasta la bye-bye, baby. Any sexy-little-thing that's a "Medium"? Gone.

So far, I hear no complaints from my honey even though he

once proclaimed perfect my 34Cs—"a nice, perky handful." He is silent about my matronly rack. The way it fills out blouses, sweaters, and lingerie; the way it weighs down a bodice and reveals too much cleavage or pulls at frontal buttons. Not one word. Mum's also the word for the not-so-pretty, seamless underwire, full-coverage, full-figure bras. He is a wise man.

TWO: The Jobs of Boobs include the following: attract a mate; boost aesthetic effect; convey the life and death powers of female deities; embellish the chest; enhance a sense of self; fill a man with delight; flirt, tempt, and seduce; interact with partners as sex, fetish, and erotic objects; nurse a child; provide subjects for art (the simply nude, the suckling mother, the suckling lover, the ravaged woman, the Venus on a half shell); reward men in Muslim Paradise: voluptuous/full-breasted virgins with large, round breasts, which are not inclined to hang (oh, yeah . . . the virgins will also be non-menstruating, non-urinating, non-defecating, childfree, and possess "appetizing vaginas"); shape clothing; substitute for paint brushes; suggest femininity; supply names for mountains and restaurants; work as business assets, sexual signals, milk-squirting deadly weapons, and vehicles for drug trafficking.

THREE: Before her Boob Jobs, D. told me she suffered from low self-esteem because of how she looked during adolescence, pointing to the "ugly" middle school pictures taken before she had braces—her first augmentation. If you could see the dramatic before and after difference, you might appreciate how the ordinary experience of successful orthodontia predisposed her to the assorted aesthetic interventions that pepper her life. The thyroid medication she took not because she had thyroid disease but because it helped her lose weight. The morph into fashion freak, starting when she was a teenager, escalating as she approached middle age. Approached now. The diets. The Zone. The South Beach. The Nutrisystem. The

Jack LaLanne Juicer juices. The bioidentical anti-aging hormones. The expensive face and body creams. Clinique. Repairwear Laser Focus Wrinkle and UV Damage Corrector. Repairwear Laser Focus All Smooth Makeup. Repairwear Intensive Eye Cream. Which didn't work. Which suggested a face lift. Which suggested a Boob Job. Which wasn't enough. Which suggested another Boob Job. Which seemed to satisfy D's lover. Which seemed to satisfy D. too. Which seemed to cure her low self-esteem—for now.

FOUR: Heaven help me. My granddaughter has boobs. One day she was my sweet, little flat-chested grandchild. The next she's my sweet, grown-up and curvy grandchild. The staples of her wardrobe? Tight camis under tight t-shirts. The layers enhance rather than conceal. The necklines plunge. And she has beautiful, eye-catching cleavage. Oh. My. God.

FIVE: Famous Boob Jobs: Artemis is particularly well-endowed with about seventeen teats—or is it two teats and fifteen bull testicles? If you want your phallic arrow to fly straight and true, you cut off your right breast like Amazon warrior queen, Hippolyta. Martyr Saint Agatha of Sicily's breasts? Crushed and hacked off. Picasso dislocated his subjects' shard-like globes in *Les Demoiselles d'Avignon*. Germaine Greer burned her bra and liberated tits everywhere. Those bad, blond girls in *Austin Powers*? Their knockers sprout cannons. Lady Gaga's bazongas can shoot fireworks as well. Joan of Arc and Gwyneth Paltrow bound their bumps to look like men. Barbie had a reduction. Elizabeth Edwards had a double mastectomy. Olivia Newton John reconstructed hers. Christina Applegate lopped hers off in a pre-emptive breast cancer strike. Chastity Bono decided hers were optional, added a penis, and changed her/his name to Chaz. Porn star, Sexy Cora Berger, died during her sixth enlargement surgery (34F to a 34G), doctors telling her husband as she lay there dying, "The brain damage was too big."

SIX: My lesbian friend baked her lover a cake. We're not talking about your regular, run-of-the-mill flat cake with chocolate icing and sprinkles. No. As it happens, while scrounging around in the cupboard, she discovered heart-shaped pans once used for a Valentine's Day party. And there, inside the hearts, were the sports ball pans she'd used to try to make a baseball cake for her son's first birthday—eight years ago. Seeing the half balls upside-down in the hearts like that gave her the idea. A bikini cake. They'll make nice ta-tas, she thought. The two hearts, with a few nips and cuts, made the perfect hour-glass shape. And then, with a glob of icing on the flat side of each half-circle and two straws as anchors, my friend did her Boob Job magic. She iced the cake smooth with flesh coloring. Nude, the buxom, no-nippled torso was unnerving, but my friend wasn't yet done. There was the skimpy, blue, string-bikini bottom yet to be applied. After that, she painted a hot pink butterfly tattoo on one hip. The final debate was whether to cover the areola area with a couple of ribbon tassels or flower pasties. She finally opted for a matching bikini top, leaving the strings untied with one erect nipple exposed. The laces spelling *Just* across the upper chest and *For Fun* across the bare belly.

In a magnetic frame on the fridge is the snapshot my friend took capturing her lover's reaction to the cake. She is, of course, grinning like a Cheshire cat.

SEVEN: Tomorrow your daughter gets a Boob Job. Your baby. Just twenty-four. And she is getting a boob job because, she tells you, she is done having and nursing kids. Nursing your two adorable granddaughters obliterated her breasts. Not that she had much to begin with. And while you don't like the idea, you get it. She did not inherit your breasts. No. She inherited the small, fried egg-shaped breasts of your sister, the same breasts found on an aunt, several cousins, and one or two of your nieces; breasts that do not fill a bodice or shape a sweater without a thickly padded Wonder

Bra. Your aunt and sister reconciled themselves to their cleavage-less chests.

As far as you know, only one of the cousins could afford an enhancement, the same one who has four or five kids. The same one married to an oral surgeon and living in a high-priced Southern California community near the beach. But then, technically, your daughter shouldn't be able to afford a boob job. She is a stay-at-home mom. Her husband is the family's sole provider. Theirs is a tight budget. Yet, somehow, she has the money, having squirreled away earnings from odd jobs, like selling airbrush tattoos at Mud-Runs and 4th of July carnivals, and saving her half of income tax refunds. You're not surprised, really. Your daughter is patient and relentless when she wants something.

And she wants new boobs.

EIGHT: J. said, I want those movies out of my house. You watch them when I'm not home. You jerk off to them on the couch when I'm in bed.

Her husband said, If you watched the movies with me, maybe it wouldn't be an issue. I'd get excited; you'd get excited. Voyeurism feeds desire. Don't you know that?

J. said, It's not just that they're vulgar; it's that I'll never be porn-worthy. What real woman can compete with a perfect-bodied, submissive nympho? What happened to the eroticism of simple lovemaking?

He said, You might try bikini wax. A Boob Job. I could get you one for Christmas.

J. said, Fake boobs and boobiferous are not synonymous.

He said, Sure they are. And we'd both get the breasts we've always wanted.

NINE: Many Boob Jobs has E.

A. *A mastectomy.* The impact of the empty space hits hard.

Surprisingly unanticipated. Unexpected. E. has always worn layers, so there's no need to hide what's missing with a wardrobe change. It's just that she doesn't feel like wearing colors anymore. E. is more into black with white . . . mostly black.

B. *A reconstruction.* E. hates the prosthesis, but she wants to fill out her clothes; she wants a natural look with or without cleavage. But then the reconstruction . . . it doesn't work out as hoped . . . more hard chest mound than soft breast. Not that it matters. The fact is she can't imagine ever letting a man fondle anything on her chest again, can't imagine taking off her top for a man again, not since her husband said, I didn't think it would look like *that.*

C. *Redux.* A few years later, the cancer invades E's remaining breast. Another empty space. Less unanticipated? Less unexpected? E. can't say for sure.

Back in her hospital room, E's husband says, There was a problem; he says, The doctor closed you up.

At which point he leaves for home.

Fourteen excruciating hours later, the doctor tells E. the problem is her skin—not metastasis. She's not going to die. Not today, anyway.

D. *Another reconstruction.* E. is disappointed. The new chest mound is higher, larger, and harder than the old one. Her arm is swollen to three times its normal size. But it is her skin that causes her the greatest concern. It is thin and giving at the seams.

E. *Enhancements.* E. has made several important decisions. It's time to leave her husband, so she rents a little house and moves in alone. It's time to risk a new relationship, so she allows herself to get involved with a friend. It's time to make love again, so she does—with her blouse held firmly in place. It's not as if she's trying to fool anyone. The man knows what's under the blouse. And she's beginning to believe he won't turn away in disgust should it slip loose. But for now, he doesn't push to see what's hidden, and she doesn't offer to expose much, preferring, instead, the most extraordinary of pleasures: cuddling with him on the couch.

TEN: My eighty-something-year-old neighbor claims that sooner or later in every woman's life, boobs, the jobs of boobs, and Boob Jobs become irrelevant. Take hers, for example. She was a curvaceous 1940s bathing suit model. Movie star material—Ingrid Bergman comes to mind. But then she fell in love, got married, and had a few daughters. A typical woman of her era, she gave up her career and embraced the role of stay-at-home mom—a good thing since the pregnancies took their toll on her model's body—particularly her breasts. Hers was a happy, till-death-do-us-part marriage, and that took its toll, too. The lithe look of her model days was lost forever, evolving into a form she prefers and finds more comfortable—a home body.

 Then her husband died. She's not inclined to replace him. A few years after his death, she required a double mastectomy. She's not inclined to replace her breasts, either. She says, I'm done. There will be no more men. She says, Why conform to a self-image we cannot sustain or make work for us?

Dorianne Laux

Proofs and Theories

Either this new jacket is surprisingly warm
or I'm having a heart attack. It's either a wen
or cancer. Who wants to bother with facts?
Science is nothing next to full-blown fear.
Either the glass is half full or I'm going
to shoot myself. Either a leopard has spots
or you've got adult onset chicken pox.
Wherever you have shoes, a TV set and
a rocking chair you have spontaneous
human combustion. A silhouette
in the window is an escaped convict.
A rap on the door signals a home invasion.
Don't try to curry favor by offering
one of any number of other possibilities.
I'm sunk in the amplitude of years
of family history and a hysterical,
heretical form of desire: a ringing
in the ears is unquestionably tinnitus,
an errant clap of thunder is what set it off.
The scarlet fever I had as a child
has turned my liver iridescent, seething
with lesions, nothing left of my spleen
but a rag with a few shreds of fat.
I've scuffled over this floor long enough

to know I've got sciatica and if that's
not enough I've got radiculopathy.
I know, I've looked it up. And there's
a dome of flesh on the pad of my foot
that just doesn't look right. Indigestion,
warts, too much hair in the brush,
everywhere, every where, signs.

Elisabeth Murawski

This Morning in Winter

I climb from sleep
with nothing to lose.
Outside, the marble trees

shine. The sky's so
ordinary it's strange.
I study for age the skin

in the crook of my elbow,
lie here, stripped
of veneer, awaiting

with empty hands
the absurd bridegroom.
Oh to be trusting as a tree

in the status quo, robbed
of leaves yet supple
in the wind below zero.

Carol Smallwood

A Late Summer Diary

Day 1

Wanting off the merry-go-round, I trudge the library stairs to the 4th floor to capture the subterranean. It was summer so not many were around to interrupt the basking of books, the labels neatly marching shelf after shelf—a glorious movable feast.

The bookshelves have signs to guide, buttons to move the phalanx, every third shelf with a light like a helmet. I breathe deeply the cool air to capture the illusive scent when banished and homesick for it, wishing to be part of it like the incense of childhood Mass.

There was a moth on the carpet and I slipped it in a container carried in my purse for such rescues. There were no windows that opened so how did it get there? When driving in, I'd lined my tires so I'd run over a possum killed on the road to be sure it was killed and wondered again why wings of smashed birds move as if trying to fly.

When I put the moth on some Queen Ann's Lace at home it didn't move. I carried it to my plants, sprinkled it with water; at least the moth was now on soil—I wouldn't look tomorrow and believe it'd flown away as there were still some summer days ahead.

Day 2

The label from some shirt is still on the sidewalk as I walk to the library. There is a breeze for which I am grateful.

The 3rd floor reading room seemed waiting; the scent wasn't

that of books though and the lack of high shelving like the 4th floor made the air flow more, a coolness almost too cool. A couple by the window, young, the guy's head in headscarf, a cough from someone unseen.

The Times Literary Supplement had Sanskrit books on the back cover. To know there were such sets was reassuring even though it prompted how little I knew about life that old; to review such a world must be a rare privilege and yet 3,000 years is the width of an eyelash.

To see the earth as an ever-expanding universe turns everything irrelevant so it is best to believe the earth is the center of the universe. Women are closer to the way things are but with this reality comes a greater need for illusions.

Day 3

Websites are jotted down surreptitiously as if fearing disapproval from peering books and stuffed in my purse.

Last night a DVD on the Tower of London showed a ceremony of locking doors performed ever since a king entered unchallenged on his return to England. The ceremony is observed even on Christmas and continued during the Blitz: it is reassuring to think that since the 1300's the ceremony is performed every night at the same time and place.

Hope Kitty doesn't have another fur ball because it's hard leaving her at the vet's. My first decision after hearing I had cancer was putting her to sleep before I went and she changed then too, lost a lot of her bravado and started sitting by the house at dusk just staring west.

Heard from a Holocaust survivor. On one hand, I envy her because her loss is clear, her pain a known cause. The Holocaust, like child and marital abuse are still being denied. She could be a relative and I'd never know because none of mine would admit anything.

I go to the post office to join the throng, the business people opening the larger boxes carrying cell phones swooping in and out with little ceremony.

Another Day

Am writing while eating at Wendy's. One must eat every day but libraries should be kept in awe, special places of last resort—I've learned that it is wise, necessary, to keep what you value most at bay to dole out.

Scheduled fall class, switching an unknown lady professor for a man one. He is good and didn't want to chance the unknown and it's nice to see a male, a thinking male, 3 times a week. So much for supporting my own sex. The class is fantasy and science fiction which I've avoided, bent on truth finding—wisdom does not come with age and yet a part of me won't admit it.

I'm the only one here feasting at Wendy's except for the employees who extend good-humored smiles to a regular. Kitty didn't stay out long this morning because it was too windy. I brush her often every day till she scratches.

That front part of my house under the picture window is a problem—gravel when I moved but when weeds came I hadn't the desire to destroy them. I put in more stones and weeds still came. I took the stones out and put Snow on the Mountain to take over. Weeds still came. The lawn man sprayed to no avail and I won't call him back because wild lilies have come to join Queen Anne's lace.

September 2

It is the day before Labor Day. Time to drink my coffee instead of taking it home like spoils of war—not many around—students have gone home for the long weekend. The coffee is very good after a night of trying to sleep.

My writing is jagged because of the grains of sugar on the table—the end of the coffee is the best because sugar settles there.

Good to feel the pen when so much time is on computer keys: a pen somehow makes one feel more in control, like breadcrumbs for Hansel and Gretel.

Hospital floors come to mind with dots one follows gratefully because all the halls and doors look the same. Those polished floors, square tiles, beige, some set diagonal for style. Wish I could find that quote about style being shaped by limitation—best not to remember the whole file wiped out trying to change one quote.

Another hot flash from post-chemo pills. I wonder what hall my uterus traveled for disposal and imagine a long line of red circus dots. The surgeon in scrubs had been nibbling fruitcake when I was wheeled in the day before Christmas. The next day my tray had an evergreen sprig tied in red which I threw across the room—the aide called it a hormone thing.

My breasts were removed at another hospital but the floors were still beige and the white sheets also spotted with red.

We should dwell in the moment but only children can. And in diaries one does not have to apologize.

Labor Day

When did Labor Day begin? In these days of globalization, what would the founder(s) think? It is a different playing field and I am lucky to be independent now after being raised when women were primarily housewives. My daughter will rejoin the work force when her youngest starts school, and I told her to get a Superwoman cape, but she had no idea what I meant and just rolled her eyes with a skeptical smile.

Dorianne Laux

Mother's Day

I passed through the narrow hills
of my mother's hips one cold morning
and never looked back, until now, clipping
her tough toenails the yellow of blanched corn,
sitting with her on the bed's edge,
combing out the tuft of hair at the crown
where it ratted up as she slept, her thumbs
locked into her fists, a gesture as old
as she is, her bald knees fallen together
beneath a blue nightgown. The stroke

took whole pages of words, random years
torn from the calendar, the names of roses
leaning out over her driveway: Cadenza,
Great Western, American Beauty. She can't
think, can't drink her morning tea, do her
crossword puzzle in ink. She's afraid
of everything, the sound of the front door
opening, light falling through the blinds—
she pulls her legs up so the bright bars
won't touch her feet. I help her

with the buttons on her sweater. She looks
hard at me and says the word sleeve.

Exactly, I tell her and her face relaxes
for the first time in weeks. I lie down
next to her on the flowered sheets and tell her
a story about the day she was born, head
first into a hard world: The Great Depression,
shanties, Hoovervilles, railroads and unions.
I tell her about Amelia Earhart and she asks

Air? and points to the ceiling. Asks Heart?
and points to her chest. Yes, I say. I sing
Cole Porter songs, Brother, Can You Spare
a Dime. When I recite lines from Gone
with the Wind she sits up and says Potatoes!
and I say, Right again. I read her Sandburg,
some Frost, and she closes her eyes. I say yes,
yes, and tuck her in. It's summer. She's tired.
No one knows where she's been.

Dorianne Laux

Lost in Costco

Our mother wandered the aisles in the city
of canned goods and 30 lb. sacks
of dog food, mountains of sweat pants
and cheap jeans, open bins of discounted CDs.
She rested for a moment on the edge
of a bed in the furniture section,
trying to remember if it was time to sleep,
then headed off to garden supplies
where she stared at the glazed pots, missing
her roses, the ones she planted
outside the house she had to sell with the tree
she wanted to be buried under, her ashes
sealed in a See's Candy tin. We found her
on a piano bench, her purse beside her
like a canvas familiar, her fingers
running over the keys, playing the songs
she remembered, taking requests from the crowd
gathered under the buzzing florescent lights.
Faking it, picking out the tunes, striking
a chord like she'd do when we were young
and she'd say sing it to me and we'd hum
a few bars: pop songs and top forty hits,
TV theme songs or chewing gum jingles,

our high, sweet voices giving her
so very little to go on.

Lauren B. Davis

Breaking Down

I hold my mother's hand as I smooth lotion onto her skin. I keep an impassive smile on my face, for I can feel her eyes on me, looking for clues. Her arm is textured like the brittle skin of onions, overlaid with cobwebs, blotched with deep purple. The veins on the back of her hand look like bloody worms. I massage her forearms and wrists—gently, gently, for the bones could tear right through if I'm not careful. Something gritty sticks to my palms. My mother's skin is pilling like an old sweater. I raise her arm and the skin flaps like soiled cotton, both elbows encrusted with thick black scabs. I am afraid if I touch them they'll peel off.

"That's nice," my mother says, her eyes half-shut, her face fallen in on itself.

My mother's skin is breaking down.

She got these wounds on her elbows even before she landed in the hospital last week. Ten days ago when I called her at her condo, where she's lived in fierce independence until now, she told me she had been in bed and used her elbows to scoot up higher towards her pillow. As she did, the skin on the arms tore open. There had been a lot of blood on the sheets, she said. I asked her, again, if she'd let me get her more help. Could the lady I hired from the home-nursing organization pop in every week to see her instead of just twice a month?

"No," she said, in that flat adamant voice I know so well.

"I don't want people poking around here. Maybe later, in the fall."

Then she changed the subject and told stories about the dogs she'd had over the years. I let it go. My mother, who has suffered from depression and a borderline personality disorder all her life, will rear up and spit like a cobra if she doesn't get what she wants, if things don't go her way. I am adopted, and I am her only child. My adoptive father died in 1992, and up until a few years ago, she still blamed him for everything wrong in her life. I have learned over the decades to hide parts of myself away from her, not to allow her access to anything she might use later to hurt me. It isn't that she withholds her love (I've learned that thanks to therapy); it's that she has very little love to give. When I started writing my first novel, *The Stubborn Season*, based in part on my relationship with her, I used to say, "The only thing worse than being around my mother is *being* my mother." By the time I finished writing the book, I understood this was not a joke. To live inside my mother's head, where the barren landscape is treacherous with perceived betrayals, slights and manipulations and where no trespass ever recedes from view, must be a lonely and frightening place. My mother's always wanted company there, and when I'm around her I spend a good deal of energy just holding my ground.

§

I put the cap back on the lotion. I resist the urge to rush to the bathroom and wash my hands. Without her noticing, I wipe them off on a tissue. I put the lotion in the top drawer of the metal cabinet next to the bed.

"Cover that over. They steal things in here."

I cover the plastic bottle with a Kleenex. My mother blinks and smiles at me. Her teeth are yellow and brown with bits of hospital food lodged near the gums. Her white and grey hair curls randomly around her ears and forehead, but is flat on the back of her head. It is sticky to the touch. Her once-fabulous high cheekbones jut out like stones beneath her red-rimmed eyes. She smells slightly yeasty, slightly sour.

There is a noise, a sort of snort, from the woman behind the curtain in the next bed, and then she starts snoring, loud as a rumbling dump truck.

My mother presses her lips together in an expression of suppressed anger I know well. "I hope I won't have to stay with that one, that one there, the one—she's, it's like that with the grocers, no, not the cats, when you go, want . . ." She makes fists of her hands and shakes them by her head in frustration. "Oh, shit," she says.

"It's okay, Mum. It's all right."

"They're putting something in my food you know. I don't like that."

"They're not putting anything in your food."

"Oh, yes they are!"

"They're giving you some pills."

"That's what I mean. I don't want them."

"You're malnourished, Mum, and you need to take the pills to help you absorb the vitamins in your food so you can heal and get strong."

My mother has never weighed more than 100 pounds, but now she's less than 90 pounds. When My Best Beloved asked her why she wasn't eating, she just smiled and said she didn't know. In her condo we found the charred evidence of a burned plastic plate in the microwave. The fridge was half-full of moldering, liquefied vegetables, milk past its sell-by date, packets of almonds and apricots neatly wrapped but bought more than five years ago. The cupboards bulged with old cake mixes, enormous boxes of cereal, and thirty-five rolls of Saran-Wrap. In the rag-and-bone "sewing room" where she spent most of her time not sewing any longer but sitting in front of the television, I found the wax-paper lining bag from a cereal box filled with what might once have been grapes and leaves of some sort.

My Best Beloved and I flew up to see her just a month ago for her 90th birthday. How did we miss this? Why didn't we think to look past the more-or-less clean surfaces?

She looks out the window. "Oh, all right. I'll take the pills. For you."

I don't tell her the pills are, in fact, anti-psychotics. An hour from now she won't remember anyway. She's had a series of vascular brain "events"—transient ischemic attacks—and her short-term recall is shot. For example, she doesn't remember that yesterday the nurses found her with her hands around her roommate's throat.

My mother's mind is breaking down.

§

It is evening now and I am changing my mother from her day clothes into her pajamas. The woman who swore she'd kill herself if she ever lost her privacy stands beside the bed and lets her pants and her underwear drop to the floor. I have never, to my recollection, seen my mother naked. Not completely. She has, during periods when her depression or mania was acute, insisted on showing me parts of her body—her stomach, her back, her hips—standing within inches of my face and pulling up her shirt or pulling down her pants so I could assure her that no, it didn't look as though she had cancer, or ringworm, or shingles, or whatever she was paranoid about at the moment. Sometimes she repeated this over and over until I yelled at her to stop it, please, stop it. You don't have cancer for God's sake. Often she jammed the bathroom door so it would not lock or close properly so she could (and would) walk in on me while I was using it. (I learned to always check for such booby-traps and dismantle them.) I have worked so hard to keep a psychologically safe distance . . . and yet now, there is nothing to do but pray. I do pray, as I've been praying since I first got the call telling me my mother needed to be admitted to hospital. *Let me, oh Lord, forget everything but compassion. Let me, oh God, do, think, feel, only what is for her good and for my good and for your greater good. Dear God, be with us here, be with us now.* Her legs are those of a battered, wizened crow. Papery brown-and-red-blotched skin hangs. The thighs are withered, little more than rag-wrapped twigs. I want to look away, but I can't for fear she will fall. Her blouse covers her sex, and I nearly weep with gratitude at being spared that. I notice her underpants are not clean. Brown marks. She slips off her blouse. Her bra hangs over her breasts, not supporting them. I cannot look at her breasts. I cannot. The bra is so old the elastic is utterly worn out. I unhook the clasps and try to see what size it is, for I'll have to buy her a new one. The tag is faded and unreadable. I slip her pajama top over her head. It is sleeveless and pink and frilly and her poor tattered arms are a cruel joke in this girlish garment.

Nurses and aides walk in and out of the room, tending to other patients on the far side of a partition. Won't anyone please come here and help? Please, someone come and help. No one does, of course. I am my mother's family. I am the one. "Come on," I say. "Let's get you into bed."

"I'm tired," she says.

We spend a few moments in an awkward dance getting her settled. She looks at me blankly, ill at ease now there is no more busy-work to be done. Perhaps she's not quite sure who I am, or where she is, or why I'm here, or why she is. I ask her if she wants me to turn the television on.

She nods, "That would be okay."

I turn it to one of the bloody, car-chase-and-gun-battle shows she likes. (Sam Peckinpah is her favorite director. Her favorite film is "Straw Dogs.") On the screen a battered young woman lies on an autopsy table. The knife cuts and tubes go in with amplified squelching noises. The scene shifts to someone ambushing someone else. Fists and bone-crunching punches. Men run through a warehouse and guns fire.

174

"I don't think I like this," my mother says.

"But you've always liked this show," I say. "It's one of your favorites."

"I think that's changed," she says, her sparse brows drawn down. She's puzzled, too.

"Well, then. Off it goes."

We sit quietly in the twilight room. I take her hand and for a horrible moment I imagine her skin might slip off like a glove. I don't want to cry. I have a few liver spots on the back of my own hands now, and the veins are ropier than they were a few years ago. I fight a sudden urge to moisturize. "You gave us a scare you know."

"Yeah, I guess I did," she says.

"Do you remember doing a runner?" I make it sound as though it's a joke.

"Me?" She grins like a mischievous apple doll.

"You bet. The other night you got yourself dressed, coat and purse and everything. They found you in the lobby heading for the door and out onto the street."

"Really?"

"You were truckin'!"

She laughs as I imitate her determined walk, neck forward, arms pumping, the mad-hen expression of a pouting child.

"I don't think I'll do that again. I know I need to be here." She points behind me. "You know, I look out the window and this is the first day it looks right, not really right but a little more."

I look out the window. The sun has almost set, but the light still flickers on the lake, even with the first stars glinting in the charcoal sky. "What do you mean? How did it look before?"

Even the sounds in the hall have gone quiet now. She struggles to find the words. "I don't know. Not real. And I think I saw my mother—" She makes motions with her hands. "—working on something."

"Ah, so you've been seeing Grandma."

175

"I guess so." She plucks and fidgets with the sheet for a moment, and then looks up at me. "Now what will happen? Where will I live?"

"I don't know yet. But we'll make sure it will be somewhere nice. You know you can't go home again, don't you?"

"I know that. It's been so long since I was there."

The woman in the next bed begins snoring again. It sounds like the death-rattle of a freight train. My mother glares at the curtain separating the beds and whispers, "She's awful."

"She is," I say. "But Mum, do you remember you got very mad at her?"

"I did?" Her eyes are wide.

"You did. The nurse found you with her. You had your hands on her."

"I *did?*"

"I'm afraid so." The noise from the next bed is so dreadful I can see how someone might get strangled.

My mother bites her bottom lip. "Did I hurt her? I didn't hurt her, did I?"

"No, but you might have. You can't do that, Mum. You can't lay hands on anyone else." I don't know why I'm saying this. She won't remember, but somehow I need to hear her say she doesn't want to hurt anyone, that she didn't mean to hurt anyone. Because really, she can't help it, can she? She's never been able to help it.

"I think I've been very angry the past few days, haven't I?"

"I think you have been."

"Isn't it funny. Your mind does things. And you're not there."

"It must be frightening."

She shrugs as though she doesn't understand the question. She keeps hold of my hand.

"It's going to be okay, Mum. All you have to do now is let people take care of you."

176

"That'll be nice."

It dawns on me then that all my mother's life she's fought against whatever she perceived to be the worst thing that could happen. She battled my father's drinking and philandering. He did stop drinking twenty-five years before he died, but she never felt she'd won that battle because she couldn't forget. She then lived in terror he'd die and leave her alone, which he did, and up until about a year ago, when she took her first mini-stroke, she complained about that every time we spoke. I should have known when she stopped complaining about him something was wrong. She battled against moving from her house into a condo, but when she finally did, she forgot how hard she'd fought against it and loved her new home. Yesterday, in her home, I found hundreds of clippings from newspapers and magazines: *Warning signs of cancer/stroke/heart attack! Eat grapefruit/cranberries/bran/kale/blueberries, etc., etc., to avoid cancer!* Every drawer was crammed with them. They were posted inside every cabinet, stacked high on every table and counter and footstool. Articles on diabetes, cholesterol, vascular disease, arthritis, back problems, constipation, and urinary tract infections. She stockpiled vitamins and herbal remedies, some of them going back years. The shower is unusable because it's filled with bottles of green tea concentrate, lineaments and salves (some dating from the 1930s) cranberry tablets, fish oil capsules, various and sundry sleeping medications like melatonin and valerian, St. John's wort, and more bran and toilet paper than you'd think a constipated army could use. And this from a woman who never spent a day in hospital until last week, a woman whose only prescribed medication was cortisone cream for arthritis in her right thumb. The war's over. Mum lost. There's nothing left to fight. I used to say a stake through the heart couldn't kill my mother. I may, however, be wrong about that.

The woman in the bed behind the curtain has stopped snoring quite so loudly. My mother squeezes my hand and says, "I'm tired."

"Do you want me to go and let you get some sleep?"

"That would be okay."

I hug my bird-twig mother. Her hair smells greasy, her skin unwashed. I feel her ribs and her shoulder blades, as her skin slips over the bones. My throat closes over. My eyes burn.

"I love you," I say.

"I love you, too," she says, and pats my back. "My wee girl."

Elisabeth Murawski

as I grow old

I have come to know when to brush crumbs from his vest
when to tighten the cummerbund

the puppet movement of brother death
in black and white evening suit he takes off

his hat does that jerking bow of the ambassador
s'il vous plait bone on bone clicking

and rocking the faces carved into the wall
mildly looking on not hearing me cry out

as I touch the dark he comes from
rooting for applause

and it is true this chill comes from within
the night dispelled by one candle

fights to take hold wherever the earth begins
and I close my eyes I close my eyes a baby in my arms

the current taking me waking me
from the dream I am naked in Barcelona

Jan Eliot

Well Seasoned

Molly Giles

Where Have All the Old Ladies Gone?

They used to be everywhere. One sat on every front porch, park bench, and bus stop of the town I grew up in. One watched from the front window of every house; one talked to another over every back yard fence. They stood behind the counters of the dime stores, drug stores, corner markets, florists, bookstores, and soda fountains. They taught every class in the grammar school. The library belonged to them. So did the churches. They ran the beauty shops. They operated the telephones. You could not take a music lesson without going to one of them. You could not make a bank deposit. You could not buy a stamp.

That was sixty years ago, when I was a child. I thought old ladies ruled the world.

Each one was different. Each one was alike. They all wore the same clothes: black shoes that laced, heavy dust-colored hose, hand-knit cardigans, silky dresses with hems that drooped. Rubber girdles. Veiled hats with feathers. Fur boas. They all carried pocketbooks and when they pulled the keys out of their pocketbooks they opened their doors onto the same sort of room: dim, clean, with an African violet near the radiator, a sepia photograph of someone dead on the desk, a pimpled milk-glass figurine of Cinderella's hollow slipper on the bric-a-brac shelf. They kept bowls of sweets—ribbon candy, lemon drops, green and white striped peppermints—on their coffee tables. None of them ate the candy.

Their names began with Miss or Mrs. They often called each other Miss or Mrs. Their first names, linked, formed a gentle alphabet: Addie, Bessie, Clara, Dot, Edith, Fanny, Gertrude, Hazel, Ivy, Jewel, Kitty, Leila, Mabel, Nola, Opal, Phoebe, Queenie, Ruby, Stella, Theodora, Ursula, Violet, Wilma, Xenia, Yolanda, Zelda. They used these names at the tables where they played against each other in contract bridge, canasta, and mah jong. They used these names in the basement restaurants of the department stores where they gathered to eat chicken pot pie and scoops of Neapolitan ice cream from stainless steel goblets. Their dentures clicked and some of the bolder ones, the ones with full sets of false teeth, bit into the ice cream showily and chewed, unmindful of the cold. Their voices, talking to each other, were harsh and hilarious.

They talked about train trips and movie stars and radio shows and yardage sales and the few relatives—rarely husbands—they were proud of. They talked about their illnesses. They were often ill, their bodies bent, bow-legged, breakable, subject to mysterious catarrhs, goiters, dropsies. Their skin was pale and delicate as plum petals, marbled with blotches, mustaches, warts, chin hairs, liver spots. Moles the size of pencil erasers hung off their lids and upper lids.

They didn't care. Their eyes were bright, magnified behind thick glasses or beaming out unaided from beneath brows that had either been plucked and penciled to improbable arches or left in a tangle. Their cheeks were softly wrinkled and rouged. Their hair was either white or gray or came in colors from a paint box: apricot, lilac, pitch black, blue. Sometimes their hair was skewered with sharp thin wires and caged inside a filmy net that looked like something insects might hatch from; sometimes it was tucked under a turban, a babushka, a snood. At night their hair floated down free and glowed like a ghost girl's.

They got up early.

They went to bed late.

They moved around the house where the rest of us were sleeping in long flannel nightgowns that smelled like Vicks Vapo-Rub. They sighed and sipped hot water with lemon juice. Even at night their hands smelled like soup, their breath like sour tea. Their bellies smelled like baby talcum, their bosoms like funeral flowers—the rose, gardenia, violet, and lilac scents they sprinkled on stained handkerchiefs and tucked inside their brassiere straps all day. Their armpits were rank with faint sweat, their feet smelled like everyone else's, and an interesting rot came from their flanks when they crossed and uncrossed their beautiful blue-veined legs.

By dawn they were already in the kitchen. They cooked all day. Boiled green beans with gray slabs of bacon. Deep-fat fried chicken with blood at the bone. Sugary pie crusts. Watery custards. Milk toast. Aspics. Hard little lard cookies. Livers and tongues.

They were not good cooks.

No one could say this, except other old ladies. Other old ladies could say anything they pleased, about themselves, about each other, about the President of the United States, and about you. Old ladies *saw* you, when you were a child. They saw you in ways your peers and parents did not. They were not fooled by your dimples and curls. They looked right inside to something called your "character." They saw that your character was unformed and basically vile but salvageable and they believed that with a strict application of effort and will you could still become worthwhile, someday. They saw you had potential.

Because they believed in you—because they offered that great and terrible courtesy—you tried to measure up. You washed your neck and scrubbed your elbows. You stood up straight, kept your napkin in your lap, chewed with your mouth closed and did not pick your nose in public. You cleaned your side of your room, kicked your sister covertly, did your homework, double-checked your sums, said your prayers, and included them in it. You made way for them on the sidewalk. You offered them your seat on the bus. You helped them cross the street. Even though they acted as if they were helping you.

Some of them were witches. Some of them were saints. But most of them were simply the best friends you had.

I would have been lost without the old ladies of my childhood. Miss Buck taught me to read from the comics before I was four. Her maiden sister, The Other Miss Buck, taught me to tell time on a grandfather clock. Mrs. Istin made me paper dolls from the Montgomery Ward catalogue and taught me to knit with kitchen twine and two pencils. Mrs. Cotter took me rowing on the small city lake. Great Aunt Ethel took me to the Ice Follies. Great Aunt Rose took me to the ballet. Mrs. Brown, who wore a body cast, taught me to can-can. Mrs. Shippy taught me how to spell Mississippi. One of my grandmothers let me drink watered rose wine with dinner. The other grandmother sat by my bed when I was sick and made up stories about every square in my counterpane. In the white square we rode polar bears through the Arctic, in the green we camped under redwoods, in the blue we sailed the cold Pacific.

This grandmother was the love of my life. Shy, restless, she never stood still long enough for a formal portrait, but I keep a snapshot of her on my office wall. She is dressed for Easter in a slippery ill-fitting brown and white dress and she is wearing a brown hat that squats like a brood hen on top of her bad gray perm. Her shoulders sag, as does her bust. Her stomach shelves out. Her glasses are crooked. She is wearing crystal earrings and a crystal necklace; this set, which I own now, she told me came from the chandelier of a French chateau. Elves gathered it, she said, and gave it to her so she could give it to me. Her feet, deformed by bunions, are encased in orthopedic boats. Her bare arms are heavy and slack; her watch cuts into the flesh of her wrist; her rings can't come off. Her face is downcast but her eyes flash up at the camera, bright, proud, and mischievous. And the smile that exposes her badly spaced, coffee-stained teeth is so genuine that my heart bows before it even now.

Her own heart was already burdened by then, her pulse slowed by long years of widowhood, her arteries clogged from gravies and cream pies, her blood pressure soaring from the daily demands of a menial job, her sciatica screaming, her arthritis a smoldering coal on each joint.

She was my age.

Only I'm not old. I wear jeans and lacy camisoles and cowboy boots. Sun block, moisturizers, facials, and retin-A have helped preserve my skin. Contact lenses have camouflaged the need for glasses. My teeth have been straightened, my hair has been curled, and both have been bleached. I go to a gym, lift weights, do yoga, Pilates, and hike. I get massages when I need to, see a psychotherapist when I need to. I have a job I enjoy, many friends. I travel a lot. I fall in love often. I beat the steering wheel and sing to Al Green when I drive. I weigh less than I did at eighteen.

Friends my age aren't old either. We all look good. Some have had plastic surgery to help them look good, but most haven't needed it. Charlotte, 73, just came back from trekking through Myanmar. Jo, in her 80's, spent the last six months living on a barge in The Netherlands, researching a river. Barbara, 68, insists I take the wheel of her new Jaguar, and counsels as I edge down a steep stretch of coast highway, "Don't use the brake, honey, don't use the brake." Kate, 76, teaches yoga. Gina, ageless, accepting a national award for her latest book, stands at the microphone and stammers, in a young girl's voice, "I'm not ready." Susan, 60, recovering from a bout of colon cancer, jumped on a Norwegian freighter, sailed around the world, and ended up marrying the ship's chief engineer. Eve, 68, just won her umpteenth decathlon. Esther, 80, is building a back deck on her house by herself. Betty, 58, came back from Egypt with a 27-year-old tour guide.

"We're a different generation," I boast to my grown daughter who has come over with my grandson for dinner. I am whipping around the kitchen in my skinny jeans and ballet slippers, pulling out organic vegetables for a stir-fry.

"You are," she agrees. (She's a wonderful daughter.) She glances at the beginning pages of this article, which I have left lying on the counter, picks it up and reads out loud. "Where have all the old ladies gone?" she wonders.

"I know," my grandson beams. His eyes are dancing.

"You do?" We humor him. "Where?"

"Here! One lives right here! In YOUR house, Gramolly!"

What a lesson! Who needs it! I have seen the enemy and she is me. Only she's not an enemy and I couldn't have seen her without my contacts plus the huge magnifying glass I keep by the phone book. I throw the enoki and sustainable tofu back in the refrigerator; phone the pizza place for a Combination, Large; snatch my grandson up to shake the giggles out of him; and then follow him, still giggling, to my writing room where he settles before my computer. There, while we wait for the pizza to be delivered, he shows me how to Text and Twitter and I pretend to understand, delighted by the lights in his quick, intent, intelligent eyes. I watch his little hands continue to connect me to an iPhone and an iPad and an iPod and who knows what. Good heavens, I think. Where have all the children gone?

Alicia Ostriker

Approaching Seventy

1. Sit and watch the memory disappear
romance disappear the probability
of new adventures disappear

well isn't it beautiful
when the sun goes down
don't we all want to be where we can watch it

redden
sink to a spark
disappear

•

Your friend goes to Sri Lanka and works
for a human rights organization
in the middle of a civil war

where she too might be disappeared any time
and another friend goes to retreats
sits miserably waiting for ecstasy and ecstasy

actually comes, so many others
so many serial monogamists seeking love
some open doorway some wild furious breath

•

Please, I thought, when I first saw the paintings
De Kooning did when Alzheimer's had taken him
into its arms and he could do nothing

but paint, purely paint, transparent, please let me
make beauty like that, sometime, like an infant
that can only cry

and suckle, and shit, and sleep,
boneless, unaware, happy,
brush in hand no ego there he went

•

A field of cerise another of lime
a big curve slashes across canvas
then another and there is the lucidity

each of us secretly longs for
as if everything belonging to the other world
that we forget at birth is finally flooding

back to the man like a cold hissing tide
combers unrolling while he waits on the shore
of the sandy canvas brush in hand it comes

•

So come on, gorgeous, get yourself over
to the shore with the sleeping gulls
—does the tide rise or doesn't it

and are you or are you not willing
to rise from sleep, yes, in the dark, and patiently

go outside and wait for it

and do you know what is meant by patience
do you know what is meant by going outside
do you know what is meant by the tide

2. Now go dance
with the skeletons
feed them word meat be their slave

that worm there is hungry
that rubied iridescent beetle that fly
making a path through some sour dirt

you hairy impertinent bag of water
what do you know
about hunger

                    •

You hairy impertinent bag of water
says the fly buzzing on my windowsill
late in the fall about to die

tumbling over in its agony
leave me alone for God's sake
leave me my pitiful dignity

The day is azure and breezy there outside
yet I cannot look away from the anguished fly
on the sooty windowsill

                    •

Buzz buzz: what if you feel like tepid dishwater,
like a rusty Dodge, the fly says, you are still
a member of the privileged species

the killer species
that uses its intelligence to be
the world's butcher and poisoner

A toxic cloud floats by, alabaster and rose
go watch the salt seas rise and the earth crack
prepared to return your insult

•

So here you are with your meaningless choices
this way and that hesitating, fearful
should you tell the truth to your daughters

should you forgive your husband how boring
shouldn't you spend more time
trying to heal the world

if you would only recognize
you are no more than that fly
or that cloud

•

Everything would change, you would find yourself
illuminated from within like a paper lantern
carried by a whore in a Paris street fair

or like a dragon kite you would fly in a high wind
and be pulled back to earth by a string
in a child's hands, or you would be cactus

blooming blood-orange in sand, or monsoon charging across
a grateful subcontinent, or lava plunging
over old cinders to the seething sea

3.   Espresso bubbles, I shout
Breakfast in a minute up the stairs
he comes down robed, we have

coffee, toast, cherry tomatoes, cheese,
fish, juice, almond pastry, the *Herald*
Tribune then the long busy day then evening

lying in the tub after a smoke I remark
economics doesn't interest me
the three things I care about are individual

human lives, then art and beauty
then politics and cultural history and mythology
I'm thinking: apart from the personal stuff

on the other side of the tub my rational man
says truth then fun then honor, by honor he means
both reputation and doing what is right

head to foot we recline in the warm steam
while I remember a few summers ago
the tangy peachy cool night air

that blew in through the bathroom window
as we stood in the tub looking out
side by side trying to locate the comet

with the double tail, ah there it was
off to northwest over the neighbors' charcoal trees
difficult to see, like the lightest pencil touch

Elisabeth Murawski

The Octogenarians

These women speak to themselves.
They have stopped cooking their meals.
In the dark daylight they save on electric bills.
They look for letters and pray,
in harsh voices that can be overheard,
for their survivors. They are past
annoyance at the noise of children.
They have electric ears they forget to use.

These women read the large-type versions
of Reader's Digest and the Bible, hand-magnify
the news. A blaring radio takes the place of TV.
They have lost all their favorite shows,
gained wardrobes of slippers and sweaters,
nightgowns and robes. They return,
to the children who have moved away,
pictures and yearbooks, forgotten souvenirs.

By all that is holy, these women corner
the listener, fill the air with woes
respectful of their age. They stand on balconies
looking down through the haze
on white trellises, climbed trees. Their windows
creak open to the sun. They prod with gnarled fingers

both rose and thorn, and come away smitten by touch,
their swollen hearts slowed to a footfall,
a muffled drum.

Abby Frucht

Photo by John Iwata

Friday, Tuesday, Scarday, Wednesday

My first scars came from chicken pox, but the next scar came from a fall off a rope swing in Bobby Wall's yard. Bobby was the neighbor boy. His favorite game was to toss his new toy trucks into the air—new trucks with lavish price tags—and smash them with a baseball bat on their way down. His second favorite game was to line us up, shoot us, and decide **... Scars often come in handy for identification purposes, like in ...** who died the best. But on this day he wasn't home. I was alone in the scrappy patch of woods when I climbed onto the rope swing, and alone when, bloodied, I ran home. Later, we trooped back into the woods to collect the rock I fell on, for a memento. The rock resembled the slate mask that decorated our parents' living room wall, a mask darker than a porthole, the nose kin to the groove that bisected the rock, a groove that, if you hefted the rock and turned it sideways, carved out the shape of a letter K. Our parents were on one of their cruises that week, so it was Mrs. Krebs, our long-widowed babysitter, who decided that my head "laceration," as she called it, required medical attention. The kindly Mrs. Krebs, about whom I have written in one of my stories, had once been a nurse, so she fussed not at all at the sight of my young face dripping with blood. "Head wounds always look the worst," she explained as she drove us three sisters to the hospital. By the time they'd laid me down on my belly on a table and covered my head with a flap of starched cloth, the way you'd calm a pet bird, I was already perfectly happy to be there, feeling the gentle pull of the razor and then the scritch of the thread being needled back and forth. I could smell the latex gloves, and I heard my dad's name being whispered by the nurses, since he was the surgeon's colleague there at Huntington Hospital. Dad was such a gentleman, the nurses said. Feeling separate from my self, but at the same time, acutely present, I kept my eyes open inside the white tent. The surgeon promised me a scar, but that it would be hidden under my hair. Not long after Mom and Dad returned from their cruise, Mrs. Krebs met a widower, also in his sixties, and was engaged to be married. "He doesn't know the first thing about cooking!" she said. Giddy with pride, she tied her aprons with an extra flourish and took to standing at the window tapping gently at the glass with a wooden spoon, as if to greet each new crocus into the world. My head wound didn't heal as had been expected. Instead it began to fester and ooze, and not even the fancier doctors in New York City were able to identify the cause of the infection, which had been mailed to them in a Petri dish. We were instructed to soak the wound for twenty minutes, five times daily, with a cloth soaked in water milky with sour medicines. Bent forward at the waist, I pressed my face into the coolness of the bathroom counter while Dad squeezed out the washcloth, spread it flat over the wound so it dripped past my ears, and took a seat on the toilet to read aloud to me from the Miss Pickerell series. It **... Homer's Odyssey when Odysseus returns ...** was fun to be the object of Dad's professional attention for so many long periods of time each day, the counter smooth against my cheek, my scalp tickled by the warmth, and then the cooling, of the water. Each time after soaking, the area was to be swabbed in iodine and bandaged Civil War style, the gauze wrapped twice around my head, the iodine bleeding through it. "Wah happen to U kid?" a boy at school always asked. Today the scar feels like a blob of wax, but when my son peels the curls away to tell me what he sees, he finds that it looks like a letter K. Mrs. Krebs' fiancé died of a heart attack before they were married, after which we hardly saw her again. Dad has Alzheimer's now. When the woman who sits with him visits with her toddlers, he believes he is **... home, where he is recognized by ...** the toddlers' babysitter. My third scar came from waterskiing. I was thirteen. It was my first and last attempt. I never got to the skiing part of **... his nurse, Euryclea, ...** water skiing. The boat was driven by three boys my age whose voices were still changing. There were the twins, Jimmy and Johnnie, and their gawky friend, Joey. I gripped the tow bar like they taught me and braced myself against the revving of the motor. When the boat took off, the top of my swim suit popped apart, exposing my breasts. The boys flew into laughter, their voices cracking, and the ski flipped out from under me, scraping a tidy groove in my shin. I have never understood the whole pouring-saltwater-onto-wounds idea, since I found the effect of the salt water to be bracing, vivifying. The scar on my shin, like my chicken pox scars, which left two blurry shapes just over one hipbone, continues to cling to the merest assertion of its unremarkable existence, like a fog light barely visible amid the fog. Soon after the water-skiing episode, I began going steady with Johnnie, the more blushing of the twins, whose handsome older brother, Donald, would die in a car wreck that same year while on a cross-country road trip with one of his friends. Later I lay snuggling with Johnnie up in his room, listening to Credence Clearwater Revival, when the doorbell rang downstairs. It was Rick, the driver of the car in which Donald had been a passenger. Johnnie's parents, hoarsely screaming, met Rick at the door. IF IT WASN'T FOR YOU HE'D BE HERE NOW WHAT DID WE SAY WE SAID WE DIDN'T WANT HIM TO GO ON YOUR TRIP WITH YOU DIDN'T WE BUT WHAT DID YOU DO YOU TOOK HIM ANYWAY IT'S NOT FAIR YOU'RE STILL STANDING HERE WE DON'T WANT YOUR APOLOGY WE DON'T WANT TO LOOK AT YOUR FACE GO AWAY AND DON'T

COME BACK. From the window we watched Rick bravely depart. Johnnie had his own scar, a fatty tumor just under the skin of his **...** **when she is washing the dust off the soles of his feet. Of course, scars may also come in handy as a means of ...** brow. I liked to gently touch the squishy contours of the tumor while Johnnie's bashful fingertips roamed the top of my blouse. My next scars came from childbearing, but my fifth scar came from a hysterectomy. There wasn't a cancer, only some tumors and cysts and things. On the day of the hysterectomy, just two months after September 11, 2001, an American Airlines plane carrying mainly Dominican passengers would crash into The Rockaways section of Queens. 265 people died. A blackened crater strewn with luggage replaced four houses. I lay on the surgery prep bed watching reporters fight smoke and debris in the slashed-out neighborhood on TV, the lovely names of the dead—Oneida, Selene, Hipolito, Josefina, Ubencia, Xiomara, Petronila, Sobeira, Lasar, Altagracia, Teofilo, Whilman, Danilo— not yet released. A nun swept into the prep room and offered to lead me in prayer for the success of my surgery. I **... disguise. In literature, scars ...** demurred. I have no belief in God, and nor did I harbor any shadow of grief over the loss of my reproductive capacity, since I already had my boys. My friend, Kathleen, who had just met the man who would become her husband, sat with me in the prep room and later in recovery. As to whether the plane carrying the Dominicans went down as the result of a terrorist attack, it looked like it didn't. Instead, it looked like the crash had to do with rudders. My bladder and vagina were punctured during the hysterectomy, an accident about which I have already written too many essays. Urine gushed out. A doctor famous for fixing such fistulas repaired it five months later. I feel the numbness, then the burn, then the ache of that scar whenever Chuck and I make love, which happens mainly on Sundays now that we've grown so lazy about lovemaking if not about **... are frequently equated with ...** love. Neither the ache nor the numbness are necessarily entirely antithetical to **... deeds, but it is generally only ...** pleasure. It's important that we speak the names of the dead, or rather broadcast the names of the people once living. Chuck doesn't notice my pain during lovemaking; in fact, he often mistakes it for moans of praise. I will not hurt his feelings by telling him so. Four years after my fistula repair, Kathleen's new husband, John, who had been diagnosed with pancreatic cancer, found her a dog, Sofia, to be her companion once he was gone. One day while John lay napping, Kathleen brought over Sofia to play with our Golden Retriever, Ike. Of Sofia, little was known. They had found her at the shelter. Of a girlish age, she had an air of uncelebrated decorum, as if she'd secretly earned fourth place at Westminster Kennel Club Show. She and Ike began their play date by jumping on, then off a blue trunk containing woolens in our living room. First Ike leapt onto it, then Sofia, then Ike jumped off it, then Sofia, then Ike jumped back up again, Sofia followed, Ike jumped off and so on, like a Bop-Go-Round. "I called John's son and said if you don't get to Wisconsin to see your dad tomorrow it's going to be too late," Kathleen repeated, since in her grief and disarray she couldn't stop rehashing things, not even the things I had heard firsthand, like the phone calls to John's grown children she'd made in the hospital lobby the day of John's prognosis. "I told him six weeks isn't something you postpone." The blue trunk was disproportionate, higher than wide, with King-Arthur-style wrought-iron adornments. Sofia flipped onto her back on the carpet, allowing Ike to straddle her before their game got the better of him again. He leaped back up to the top of the trunk, wagged his tail, jumped back down, sniffed at Sofia's pink underside and leapt back up again. "John told me I looked fat in my red dress. He wants to die at home, people drop by, I serve food, I eat. His daughter will be flying in this weekend. Will you meet her at the airport?" I promised I would. Ike jumped off the trunk again, ignoring Sofia this time before jumping back up. She'd been lying awfully quietly for what was starting to seem like an awfully long time even for a ladylike dog at play. Our yellow tea kettle sang. Chuck had painted the trunk blue years before I met him, but it was my woolens in it. There were sweaters, mittens, hats, an unwearable pair of cuffed wool shorts from Banana Republic to be worn with **… the men who have them, like from duels, …** brown cable-knit tights. "She's been lying there an awfully long time," I ventured. As we stared at the dog, her tongue turned black. When John was wakened from his nap and came over to see, we told him what the vet had said on the phone: you know a dog is dead when its tongue turns black. "We're having more than our share of death this spring," John remarked. Chuck buried Sofia wrapped in a blanket on land up north, where the other dogs—Tyler, Taylor, and Nixon—lie buried. A prickly wreath, bleached nearly transparent, hangs crooked on one of sixty-five thousand trees. We snowshoe there in winters, dog treats in our pockets, a bottle of wine and two cups in the backpack. My sixth scars come from a dermatological condition so difficult to explain **… wars, and other things to be boasted about. …** that my doctor only squints and shakes his head. "They won't hurt, they won't itch, they'll go away for a while and then they'll come back," he says, aiming an ocular scope at the lesions, which resemble whorled groupings of islands viewed from high up in a helicopter. "It's called granuloma annulare. There's no known cause and it's never contagious. It's thought to be an autoimmune response, but even that's not clear," he said. "So I am fighting against my own **… Tattoos are scars, as are …** skin," I say. "Something like that," the doctor says. Though one of the lesions looks like ringworm, the one on my hand could as well be a burn from an oven coil. I don't remember when the lesions first made their appearance, but I know that I was sleeping in an earlier bed, not the king-size bed I share with Chuck, for which he traded his dad in exchange for a double when Chuck's mom, Louise, went into the nursing home. The king bed has a wood frame that Chuck painted **… piercings. These have cosmetic as well as ritual …** a contemplative shade of red.

"That part of my life is over," Norb said, explaining the trade. Day after day he drove across town to where Louise lay curled in the nursing home, and after she died he clipped a portrait of a lady from the local town paper, a lady who looked as Louise might have looked had she grown old with Norb the way we all wished she had, the flipped hair silver above sensible sleeves. Norb keeps the clipping on his desk for whenever he feels like losing himself in the picture of the lady, sometimes sitting in his swivel chair for an hour not swiveling, the scrap of newsprint held before him like a mirror in which he can't find himself. His estranged adopted daughter showed up out of nowhere at Louise's funeral, accompanied by two thirty-something granddaughters I'd never heard of before. When they stopped over for supper afterward, I gave them the assortment of Louise's silk scarves that Chuck kept in our closet. He was good with my giving the scarves to the granddaughters, since the granddaughters were quilters. Plus, everyone was drinking. They promised to ... **significance. The reason heavy drinking harms the liver is that it leads to the production of scar tissue around it, scars being not the direct result of injury, it turns out, but of healing. Bones ...** bring the quilt to the house and show it to me when they were finished sewing it, but they never did. Norb put both granddaughters back into his will, then took them both out again, then put them back in again. There were four other babies between Chuck's birth and the twins' adoption, Rh-positive stillborns all properly buried, only now that Louise is gone, no one knows where. The twins were adopted at five years old. Their names were Nita and Rita, but Louise renamed them Cindy and Sandy. This is one of the only facts I have of Chuck's mom: that she was a woman who changed the names of two five-year-old girls from Nita and Rita to Cindy and Sandy. Chuck requests she not be judged by it. In our cupboards are some of her meatloaf ... **can heal without compromise to their structural and functional integrity, but heart muscles are often** ... recipes. My seventh scars come from breast cancer, about which, before my own diagnosis, I once wrote a whole novel. My heroine, Isabel, whose name I misspelled unintentionally, adored her scars, but I don't adore mine. There's a big dent with peppery stipples amid my assortment of breast cancer scarring, and some blemished, crepe-papery areas, and the purple radiation burns, and some seams crudely mended, and the nipple resembling a dropped pink flower that has been stomped on by boots in a rain puddle. The best book I ever read about breast cancer is Elizabeth Edwards' *Resilience*, but the parts about cancer weren't the parts I liked best. I liked the parts about Wade, her son, and how after he died at sixteen in a car wreck, she'd used to sneak through the house opening all of the drawers in all of the dressers, only nothing was there except blouses, coins, ribbons, and underwear, never the boy she was hoping to rescue from where God had hidden him. And then she too died. Of books about death, my favorite is Janet Hobhouse's novel, *The Furies*. Hobhouse was diagnosed with cancer in the middle of writing it, and then the heroine of the novel got cancer, too, so the two of them faded and blurred and then died together, in unison. The book was left unfinished to Hobhouse's editors, who noted that: "In preparing the novel for publication the editors have made every effort to fulfill her intentions. A few passages were still in first draft, and here it has seemed preferable to allow a break in the narrative rather than include material concerning which the author was ambivalent. These are marked by three-dot ellipses: [...] In the case of the final **... weakened by scars, causing heart ...** chapter, the fragments and synopsis have been presented as they stood." Still, even in ordinary books, books not about death or dying, three-dot ellipses remind us of mortality, by marking the vast spaces to either side of the several distinct movements that make up our lives. The writer, Stanley Elkin, my fiction prof at Washington University, when already crippled by the illness that would claim him, used to tell us that all of our fledgling stories had to do with death, whether we knew it or not, and if they didn't, they sucked. He banged on the desk when he said our stories sucked, just to prove that he still had the strength to do it, his cigarette smoke ghosting the onionskin sheaves of our manuscripts.   After we graduated, a guy in the same class, John, whose wife Kathy, a poet, liked to defiantly confess to vacuuming up dropped pennies instead of picking them up and pocketing them especially when she and John were scrambling for rent money, told me what creamy, round breasts I had. "What makes you think you know that?" I asked, since John had never seen me without my clothes.   After which I wrote a one-act play about a man based on him, who lived on his hands and knees in a dog cage. That play is long gone. Maybe someday I'll stumble upon it in a box, trunk, file, or dresser drawer. When I said to Chuck, about my scarred breast smeared with ointment, "They'll never be pretty again," Chuck replied, "That's fine, Hon, as long as I'm the only one who ever gets to look at them." My eighth **... failure. Because scars contain neither hair follicles nor sweat glands, I suppose that means that if you were covered with them, you'd be bald and dead. Scars as notation, scars as ...** scar came from the Jorge Chávez International Airport in Lima, Peru, **... typography, scars as punctuation, scars as hieroglyphic, scars as recorded personal ...** when I was on my way home from visiting my son Alex just after I completed my cancer treatments. He had lived in Peru two years already, and it was my third visit. We began our adventure at my favorite little *hostal* in Lima, bussed eleven hours south to a marine sanctuary to see a lunar fjord blanketed with penguins, bussed back to Lima, then east into the Valley of Santa Eulalia on a search for the famous avocado ice cream, then north to where Alex lived in Chiclayo, a city whose every stretch of sidewalk was studded with sudden, black, rectangular potholes. After that in Cajamarca we climbed many steep hillsides marked by ancient Incan aqueducts.   My lower leg was hurting terribly the whole time, reminding me of the "leg-aches" that had kept me awake when I was a **... history. Although ...** girl. "I have a leg-ache," I'd say, waking my parents, who fed me aspirin and put

203

me back to bed. At night in my hotel room back in Chiclayo, between bouts of recording that day's events in my battered leather diary, I kicked the sore calf hard against the edge of the mattress, hoping to bang out the knot of pain, which grew only tighter, deeper, and angrier, until after some of our day trips, I'd lie for hours simply resting, happily enough, just floating along on the curious mixture of physical torment and emotional well-being. Not even the fact that we had arrived in Santa Eulalia a scant ten minutes after the last tub of avocado ice cream had been emptied put a kink in this wonderful time with my son, since instead of eating ice cream we wandered a dusty road along a valley strewn with beer gardens where motley bands played charangos under dangling paper lanterns. At the end of two weeks, with ten hours to spare at the airport in Lima before my flight left for home, I ducked into the Day Spa, deciding to pamper myself with a hair wash and a pedicure. Since it was too early before my flight to check my luggage, I piled it next to my pedicure station, unduly worried somebody might steal it. It contained only two things of value to me; a giant Peruvian milk chocolate bar which would be my anniversary gift to my parents, but which still lies uneaten in their refrigerator, and a pot of silky face cream given me by Alex's girlfriend, Jessica. I bought Jessica a necklace, but in none of the photos I've seen of her since has she been wearing it. The pedicure—the dipping of my feet into the swoosh of warm water, the clipping of the nails, the massage to my insteps, the careful application of the buffers, lotions, oils, files, and brushes—did not chase the knot of pain from my leg, nor did the long sit home on the airplane. Because it was summer, I was able to keep my feet uncovered even once I reached home, showing off the too-scarlet toenail polish, which, against the whiteness of the exam room at my post-radiation therapy appointment, resembled gashes brimming over with fresh blood. "How was your trip?" asked Dr. Xsie, who peers so deeply into the eyes of his patients it's as if he knows their destinies as well as their prognoses. His sincerity unnerves me; I tend either to stammer or gush in reply. "It was great," I answered. "It was a fabulous, fabulous, incredible time in a gorgeous, amazing country. The only thing is my leg hurts. It's been hurting the whole time. I plan on going to the YMCA this afternoon and running it out on the ... **scar tissue is made of the same protein as normal tissue, in scar tissue the protein aligns in ...** treadmill." "Oh?" asked Dr. Xsie, recalling the intricate connection between plane rides, bus trips, cancer, blood clots, stroke, and Tamoxifen, the drug given breast cancer patients against recurrence. "Where does it hurt and what does it feel like?" and then he shooed me at once to the ultrasound lab, where the tech found so much deep vein thrombosis, she wouldn't let me leave the lab except in a wheelchair, lest I dislodge a clot and perish that minute. I felt old in the wheelchair, cheated of joie de vivre in Spanish, insulted by the dreary dietary restrictions required of me by the ... **a single direction rather than by an arbitrary arrangement of fibers. Scars as evidence, scars as forensics, scars as fragmentary clues, scars as points of ...** blood thinners. Today is May 18th, 2011, nine months after my trip to Peru, the duration of a pregnancy. Peruvian toenail polish lasts far, far longer than U.S. toenail polish, and these nine months later I still won't swab off the remaining strip of polish, which resembles an incision. The only thing that bothers me is my upcoming trip to teach writing in Israel. In spite of my enjoyment of solitary plane trips, I would rather ... **intersection with the harbingers, messengers, and perpetrators of the outside world. Scars as ...** not go. I shouldn't have accepted the six-week position, for I would rather stay home, not least because somebody has died for every section of this essay, which I have intentionally typed as one endless long shape, the pieces all strung together. As for travelling alone to Israel, I would rather just sit outside with Chuck in the breeze off the lake, grilling skinless chicken, throwing tennis balls for Ike, drinking glasses of seltzer splashed with Chardonnay while listening to the wolves howling in the zoo beyond the tennis

205

courts next door. Chuck has a fresh bruise on the crown of his head that worries me, a spongy nodule amid the freckles and wisps, underneath which he is thinking of Theodore Roosevelt, since that's the biography he's currently reading, the kind of nodule you might find on the rind of a honey dew melon left for too long in the ripening bag in the kitchen. I'm reluctant to poke it, afraid of finding something other than Theodore Roosevelt's post-presidential wrangling with President Wilson's inadvisable neutrality residing underneath it, so instead I press my fingertip against the funny letter K incised into my own skull by that rock in the woods in Bobby Wall's backyard, and I discover there today a curious, uncharacteristic tenderness, a ghost of that earliest impact, like a warning never to forget letting go of that rope, and always to remember old Mrs. Krebs, whom I am certain is gone now, cooking heavenly buttered egg noodles with poppy seeds for the man she was going to marry, who couldn't even "fix his own peanut butter sandwich!" I once met a twice widowed woman whose only worry was which of her husbands she'd sleep with in Heaven. Both, she decided, since it's possible things are looser in Heaven, less cruel, more forgiving. The remainder of the scar-let Peruvian toenail polish, now that some weeks have gone by since I last wrote about it, is finally just about gone. There is only the faintest, most filamentous of ... **Cross-Stitch, scars as Chain-Stitch, scars as Crazy-Work, Pulled-Thread, Punched-Work, Cut-Work, Back-Stitch, Mediaeval, Iridescent** ... embroidery.

Dorianne Laux

Over the Hedge

We labor in the backyard, weeding,
pulling stones like tumors up
from the hardened clay, lumpy
ogre-piles of rock-clod-weed:
scare-crowish. Back to bent back,
we are tin-foil and matchstick, stooped
over our rakes like Van Gogh's long dead
Hay Makers, though maybe happier
in our work, work that brings forth
little more than a few ratty tomatoes,
knobby volunteer potatoes, the odd
renegade squash. We leave in the wild
carrots and hollow onion stalks, dead-head
the gangly rogue rose we've grown to love
like a headstrong adolescent boy.
It's mostly exercise for the quickly aging here:
fresh air, a loss of self-consciousness, to be
without thought among the reedy weeds,
brushing gnats from our eyes, pollen-
fingered, followed by bursts of orgiastic
sneezing, stopping us in our tracks.
We tug up feeder root saplings knowing
in some distant way that without us
this garden will, in a few untended years,

become a forest of oak and ash,
the lilac, thriving now, will become stunted,
shriveled, curled up like an old woman
in the deadly hemlock shade. This patch
of grass we stand in, freshly mown,
will dwindle to a few scruffy tufts,
and the porch with its new coat
of off-white paint is really nothing more
than a future ladder for the un-removable
morning glory. And the ivy will crawl down
from its banks in a slow green wave
to cover the driveway's broken shore,
then climb our shingled house, growing over
the windows we washed just last week,
one inside, one out, rags in our hands,
working circles in tandem, making
faces at each other through the glass.

Ellen Visson

Photo by Horst Tappe

O Woe Is Me . . . and There You Meta-Have it

L et us begin this Winter's Tale at the end. The final syllables of our anthology's title are *Aging*—which, indeed, always has the last word. Dear Reader. Fact: no matter what your birth date, each second is senescent. There. You are now older than when you began reading this essay. Me too. Thus, as an aging woman, I request forbearance from you (as the *aging* Dear Reader) towards the archaic, and their Apostrophes. We shall deal in this meta-essay with the verb *to write*—and the *writer*, as maturing female—later.

My second entreaty: a petition for your indulgence while I wallow in mine.

When it was suggested that I try my freckled hand at this essay, my first reaction was to bristle at the familiar slap against the putty cheek, followed by: How dare they! That's not me. Then the flood of embarrassment, the effort of acceptance all over again: Yes, that is me (reluctant aside to mirror). It's even more than me because it's almost done.

To the careful reader well-versed in Judeo-Christian tradition and Abrahamic religions, I have just confessed. Revealed myself naked (no longer an alluring sight). You, Dear Reader, have just been made a witness to many Sins:

- hubris (Greek Tragedy's golden-oldie, and top-hit on its fatal flaws' chart);

- narcissism (its namesake a self-drowning victim);

- vanity (a poor cousin to the former);

- regrets (auto-flagellation by use of mental whirligigs with mind-spikes);

- self-pity (not pretty);

- whining;

- covetousness or envy (a voracious cannibal of the inner self);

- bitterness (inevitable result of the above); with finally

- that New Age No-No, *lack of Appreciation for the Moment*—this list's only Sin of Omission, as opposed to Commission. A sole ghost, and therefore the most haunting.

Might *Appreciation for the Moment* be the alchemic formula—the mystical mantra or psycho-catalyst—to transmute *Time*, and distill it into that golden peace we all seem to seek? Might this *Gratitude for the Present* filter out the silt from our past, while abolishing those amorphous terrors of the future? (Yes, yes, taxes and death—or rather the process of taxes and death.) For if we remain in the *Moment* with *Appreciation* for it, how can we compare our past with our present; or the assumed riches and families of others to our own meager resources? How can we commit the above Sins? We cannot: even Narcissus needed an innocent instant to forget that the world he was observing was his own reflection. Might *Appreciation of the Moment* then render serenity to this particular twilight of a non-god?

Perhaps, Dear Reader, you are amoral, and don't believe in Sin, which you might define as a product of said-Abrahamic culture, from which you have bailed out. Good for you, to have eliminated all *Guilt*. Perhaps you were a secular Humanist or Agnostic, who evolved into Eastern philosophies, whizzed by the Tao, to finally plunk full-circle into Atheism. (No, that's not good enough. Many atheists retain principles, and thus can experience remorse upon breaking them.)

Perhaps then, Dear Reader, you have spiraled back to earth, crash-landed into Paganism. If you are now dancing in that merry circle, you have substituted magical *Powers* for *Repentance*; and replaced *Sin* by the appeasement of *gods*, with their *Elemental Principles*. (This nevertheless will also require cringing before *demons* and *Destruction*.)

If you are a Pagan, welcome. Your multitudes are growing. Again. And, as I understand it (correct me, *O Eddaic Odin*, if I am wrong), there exist two methodologies with which Pagans deal with their elderly women: either they venerate them as soothsayers, or they oust those useless dried-up food-consumers. Slaughter them. Leave them on glaciers to die. Those crones don't even weigh in as human sacrifices to *Odin* or *Wotan* or the druidic *Taranis,* because they are not useful enough to be missed. I would therefore put forward the hypothesis that your Paganism—and the acquiescent Judeo-Christian culture—have at last overlapped, as to attitudes towards the elderly female.

Which brings me—with my already confessed vindictive nature—back to *Appreciation of the Moment*: it might be effective, but only if it is enlivened by knowledge of the mutual knell that awaits us all. Because—whether a Believer or Atheist, Sinner or Amoral Reprobate, Agnostic or Pagan, sufferer of Scrupulosity or Anomie, Deconstructionist or Post-Structuralist or Metalinguist or Throwback Existentialist—we shall all die. Dear Reader, if you are a youngster, you might want to advance boardwalk to the final poem; or if you are morbid or kind or both, you might continue. For only the mature, morose, and compassionate can grasp this defining question:

Dear Reader, where is that moment for you on the otherwise vast continuum of your existence when that continuum physically began to shrink? Because that is the point on the line, if you have

212

experienced it, that defines when you have begun to age.

I believe that in any society (other than Amazon), this point on the line of life comes sooner for females than males. (Pagans, sharpen your Long Knives!) This defining moment—when frantic motion in search of promises and dreams slows its spin forward to wend, wistfully, towards the past—might arrive slowly. In stealth. Or it might hit you like the proverbial freight train. Dear Reader, I offer the only example I can: my own.

My survival stuns me. The first rumblings that time would begin to stop came when my husband was diagnosed with cancer—despite there having been two rainbows across the Neuchâtel landscape while driving to the doctor with two Mormon missionaries as dog-sitters for our Chihuahua and Russian wolfhound (but that is another story). This was the point on my fleshy continuum when the everyday and normal went up in a *poof.* Final contact with said-train crushing said-cranium (the weary metaphor at last pulling into the station) was when he died of it—though the cancer lived on for a few extra hours. Cancer cells, researchers tell us, are immortal.

The following is no longer self-pity but fact. Dear Reader, I watched it. Irises faded, losing their hazel symmetry to become green shards, something almost tangible draining from behind them. At that instant, I aged. I caught up with myself, as in a special effects film when all those busy little clones out there tending to business smash together to merge into one. Alone. Lonely. Losing hair. Losing estrogen. Losing muscle tone. Losing hope. Aging.

To all wives who might not yet be widows: listen up, honey. *Appreciate your moment.* Even if you are still vital and juicy; even if he is a louse who has cheated; even if he has progeny out there with other women; if he dies first, you begin to dry up, crinkle, and experience pain (arthritic or heart-branded) more intensely than ever before. Ruling out psychopaths and family-beaters, that dead other (no matter how much he done you wrong) becomes cloaked in our memory with a reverence that he could never in our conscious minds have merited during his lifetime. He becomes, despite us, beatified.

And be aware: after the condolences, the rituals and rites, after children resume lives (as well they should), Western society will eject you. A solitary female will always be *une de trop*—one too many. Forget the couples for whom were thrown so many fêtes. Widows are not suitable for dinner parties and at best are invited to conferences, cocktails, and neighborhood events. Even a career will not save her. Even fame and riches as a pop-cultural icon won't spare her. Because, though she might receive scads of invitations, she will always be perceived as a persistent chagrin in her solitary bubble. A harbinger of things to come. A reminder to us all as the finish fast approaches. Unless of course she remarries or re-partners and restarts, nearly at dotage, the whole shebang over again.

Bitterness, you accuse? Not really. Just common knowledge.

Observe, please (should you have the opportunity, for most remain hidden), the first old woman with a cane who creaks by, staring myopically through badly corrected cataracts at the ground to avoid that inevitable fall, the one that will put her out for good. Does she not know she's invisible? Of course she does.

Or look for the elderly couple that crouches past, flesh formed to one another as they hold on, the waters choppy now, the anchor lagging, the ol' heave-ho awaiting one of them (few have the luck to go together). Are they invisible? No. They are a fleet with a purpose, their sails catching wind for the sake of the other. Yes, they are agèd. But have they experienced aging? Of course. But not in the same way as someone alone, because their *repère*—their points of reference on their separate continua—remain parallel, each with the other's.

Plus, they get invited.

Conclusion: a solitary *aging woman* is not welcome in the societal pack.

Now, let us tackle this anthology's verb: *writing.*

Dear Reader, if you are an aging woman, writing can save you. It cannot secure you eternal babe-hood but it can preserve your passion. It will spare you loss of lust for living, and other things. It can provide, instead of husband or companion, parents or children, your Other. Even lots of Others.

It is said that, when Flaubert's valet on a bet announced the arrival of Madame Bovary, the writer replied: "Show her in."

Paintings:

Philippe Visson, *Tanya Deformed by her Demons*, 1969, oil on canvas, 116cm x 89cm

Philippe Visson, *The Brothers Karamozov*, 1968, oil on canvas, 195cm x 130cm

Philippe Visson, *Tanya with her Demons*, 1969, oil on canvas, 146cm x 114cm

Elisabeth Murawski

Mrs. Malloy

At 89, why *not* wear
a prom dress (rhinestone
spaghetti straps, yards
of pale blue tulle) for her
birthday photo op? See

how she twirls despite
a stapled hip (Grace
Kelly gloves, a wrist
corsage of orchids and baby's
breath, a silver clutch

to match her silver pumps).
Chin up, rheumy eyes trapped
in flesh that sags
like yesterday's balloon,
she tosses thinning

curls, with quick pink
tip of tongue licks upper
lip, and waves him
closer, closer,
she has a story to tell:

decades ago, when
a not-so-gay divorcee
lay sobbing in a heap

on the beach,
a voice broke in mid-

angst, tossed this bouquet:
You are not alone.
"It was like seeing
a great blue heron,"
she says, her face

luminous. "Consoling
as the balm of Gilead."
She points one silver
toe, hands up, hostage
to the glorious,

and he shoots the look
he's been waiting for,
catching her
in the bath, as it were,
crazy with hope.

Contributors

Renée Ashley is author of four volumes of poetry (*Salt*—Brittingham Prize in Poetry, Univ. of Wisconsin Press; *The Various Reasons of Light*; *The Revisionist's Dream*; and *Basic Heart*—X. J. Kennedy Poetry Prize, Texas Review Press) as well as two chapbooks and a novel, *Someplace Like This*. She is poetry editor of *The Literary Review* and on the faculty of Fairleigh Dickinson University's two low-residency graduate programs, the MFA in Creative Writing and the MA in Creative Writing and Literature for Educators.

Supriya Bhatnagar is the Director of Publications at the Association of Writers & Writing Programs (AWP) and the editor of *The Writer's Chronicle*. She has an MFA in nonfiction writing from George Mason University. Serving House Books published her memoir *and then there were three...* in September of 2010. Essays from this book have appeared or are forthcoming in *Perigee* and *Artful Dodge*. Her short stories have been published in *Femina* and *4Indianwoman.com*

Michelle Bitting has work forthcoming or published in *Prairie Schooner, Nimrod, Narrative, Crab Orchard Review, Passages North, Many Mountains Moving, Rattle, Linebreak,* and others. Poems have appeared online in *Poetry Daily* and *Verse Daily*. In 2007, Thomas Lux chose her full-length manuscript, *Good Friday Kiss*, as the winner of the DeNovo First Book Award and C & R Press published it in 2008. She holds an MFA in Poetry from Pacific University, Oregon.

Kelly Cherry has published twenty books of fiction, poetry, and nonfiction, eight chapbooks, and translations of two classical plays. Her most recent titles are *The Woman Who*, a collection of short stories (2010), *The Retreats of Thought: Poems* (2009), and *Girl in a Library: On Women Writers & the Writing Life* (2009). She was the first recipient of the Hanes Poetry Prize given by the Fellowship of Southern Writers for a body of work. Other awards include fellowships from the National Endowment for the Arts and the Rockefeller Foundation, the Bradley Major Achievement (Lifetime) Award, a USIS Speaker Award (The Philippines), a Distinguished Alumnus Award, three Wisconsin Arts Board fellowships, and selection as a Wisconsin Notable Author. In 2010, she was a Director's Visitor at the Institute for Advanced Study in Princeton. Currently Poet Laureate of Virginia, she is Eudora Welty Professor Emerita of English and Evjue-Bascom Professor Emerita in the Humanities at the University of Wisconsin-Madison. She and her husband live in Virginia.

Lauren B. Davis's most recent novel, *Our Daily Bread*, was named one of the "Best Books of 2011" by both *The Boston Globe* and Canada's *The Globe & Mail*. She is also the author of the bestselling and critically acclaimed novels, *The Radiant City*, a finalist for the Rogers Writers Trust Fiction Prize; and *The Stubborn Season*, chosen for the Robert Adams Lecture Series; as well as two collections of short stories, *An Unrehearsed Desire* and *Rat Medicine & Other Unlikely Curatives*. Her short fiction has been shortlisted for the CBC Literary Awards and she is the recipient of two Mid-Career Writer Sustaining grants from the Canadian Council for the Arts. Lauren reviews books for *The Globe & Mail, The Literary Review of Canada,* and *www.Truthdig.com* and she leads monthly Sharpening the Quill writing workshops in Princeton, New Jersey. For more information, please visit her website at: www.laurenbdavis.com

Jan Eliot is the creator of the internationally syndicated cartoon strip *Stone Soup*. It appears daily in over 250 newspapers throughout the United States, Canada, and beyond. Eliot began cartooning as a single working mom looking for ways to find humor in her predicament of too little time, money and patience. She sought syndication because she wanted to work from home and didn't know how slim her chances of success were. Fortunately, her naivete eventually paid off. 2011 marks 16 years of syndication for *Stone Soup*. Jan blissfully works from her home in Eugene, Oregon, and is trying to age gracefully. There are also nine *Stone Soup* cartoon collections in print, including *We'll Be Really Careful* and *Brace Yourself*, both full-color collections from Four Panel Press. Stone Soup books are also published in Portugal by Editorial Bizancio, Lisbon.

Abby Frucht's new collection of stories, *The Bell at the End of a Rope*, is forthcoming from Narrative Library. She is the author of five novels including *Licorice, Life Before Death,* and *Polly's Ghost*. Her earlier collection of stories, *Fruit of the Month*, which won the Iowa Short Fiction Prize in 1987, will soon be available in ebook form along with Abby's other books as part of Dzanc Books' new rEprint series. A recipient of two National Endowment for the Arts fellowships, a New Voices Award from Quality Paperback Book Club, several grants from the Ohio Arts Council, and the Kay W. Levin Short Nonfiction Award from the Council for Wisconsin Writers, Abby has reviewed both fiction and nonfiction nationwide and has seen her essays widely anthologized. She lives in Wisconsin, teaches at Vermont College of Fine Arts, has raised two sons, and is currently collaborating on a new novel with her friend and colleague, Laurie Alberts. See www.abbyfrucht. net

Hester L. Furey is a literary historian who teaches college-level English. She has worked for the Art Institute of Atlanta for thirteen years and has also taught at Agnes Scott College and in the Decatur City Schools. She is the editor of *Dictionary of Literary Biography 345: American Radical and Reform Writers, Second Series*. Furey is one of the foremost authorities in the United States on American radicals of the Gilded Age and Progressive Era, particularly anarchists, feminists, and free-thinkers. She has written numerous reference book entries and journal articles on figures such as Arturo Giovannitti, the Industrial Workers of the World, Mary E. Marcy, Harriet Monroe, Scott Nearing, and Cora Richmond.

Molly Giles is the author of a novel, *Iron Shoes*, and two award-winning collections of short stories, *Rough Translations* and *Creek Walk*. She teaches Fiction Writing at the University of Arkansas in Fayetteville.

Bette Lynch Husted lives and writes in Pendleton. Her works include a chapbook *After Fire* (Pudding House, 2002) and *At This Distance: Poems* (Wordcraft of Oregon, 2010). Her first collection of memoir essays *Above the Clearwater: Living on Stolen Land* (OSU Press, 2004) was a finalist for the Oregon Book Award and the WILLA Award in creative nonfiction, and a second collection is forthcoming from Plain View Press. Her poems have appeared in *The Oregonian, Runes, Natural Bridge, Passager, Windfall,* and other journals. She has been a Fishtrap Fellow and received a 2007 Oregon Arts Commission Award.

Leigh Anne Jasheway is a humor writer, motivational speaker, and stand-up comic living in Eugene, Oregon, with her two wiener dogs, four koi, and hundreds of voices in her head. She has seventeen published books, including *Not Guilty by Reason of Menopause* (Ten Speed Press, 2008), *Confessions of a Semi-Natural Woman* (Comedy Workout Publishing, 2010), and *Bed Time Stories for Dogs* (Andrews and McMeel, 1996). She was a regular columnist for *Family Circle* for years and now writes a monthly humor column for *Dash Magazine*. Her work has been included in more than two dozen anthologies, and she is the winner of the 2003 Erma Bombeck Humor Writing Award for her true story on how her first mammogram caught on fire.

Dorianne Laux's most recent collections are *The Book of Men* and *Facts about the Moon*. A finalist for the National Book Critics Circle Award, and winner of the Oregon Book Award and the Roanoke-Chowan Award for Poetry, Laux is also author of *Awake, What We Carry,* and *Smoke* from BOA Editions. She teaches poetry in the MFA Program at North Carolina State University and is founding faculty at Pacific University's Low Residency MFA Program.

As of 2011, **Ursula K. Le Guin** has published twenty-one novels, eleven volumes of short stories, four collections of essays, twelve books for children, six volumes of poetry and four of translation, and has received many awards: Hugo, Nebula, National Book Award, PEN-Malamud, etc. Her recent publications include the novel *Lavinia*, an essay collection *Cheek by Jowl*, and a collaboration with Roger Dorband, *Out Here: Poems and Images from Steens Mountain Country*. She lives in Portland, Oregon.

Clare MacQueen is a copy editor and Web designer who lives in the Pacific Northwest, where she and her husband, Gary Gibbons, build custom websites. She is also Webmaster for a handful of author and literary sites. Her nonfiction has appeared in *Best New Writing 2007*, and her short fiction in *Bricolage* and *Serving House: A Journal of Literary Arts*. Two of her essays were nominated for the Pushcart Prize. She likes to think of herself and Gary as "geeks and beeks," since they share obsessions for computers, sci-fi movies, flower gardens, and keeping honey bees in the backyard.

Alexandra Marshall has published five novels and a work of nonfiction. She has been a film critic for *The American Prospect* and a guest columnist for *The Boston Globe*, and her short stories and essays have appeared in journals including *Ploughshares, Agni, Five Points, Hunger Mountain, The Cape Cod Voice*, and *The New York Times*.

Laura McCullough is the author of several books of poetry, including her most recent book *Panic*, winner of a 2009 Kinereth Gensler Award. In addition to poetry, she writes essays, fiction, and literary memoir as well, and has been awarded two New Jersey State Arts Council Fellowships, one in prose and one in poetry. She has been awarded scholarships or fellowships from Sewanee Writers Conference, Bread Loaf Writers Conference, the Vermont Studio Center, the New Jersey State Council on the Arts, and the Nebraska Summer Writers Conference; and was a finalist for a fellowship in Creative Nonfiction at the DC Writers House. A featured performer at the 2010 Dodge Poetry Festival, she is also editing an anthology of essays by contemporary poets on the work of Stephen Dunn and is co-editing an anthology of essays on poetry and race with Reginald Dwayne Betts. She is the editor of *Mead: the Magazine of Literature and Libations* and an editor at large for *TransPortal Magazine*. She teaches in the Winter Poetry and Prose Conference in southern NJ and founded the Creative Writing Program and Visiting Writers Series at Brookdale Community College in central Jersey.

Roisin McLean has published fiction in *Perigee: Publication for the Arts, Fiction Week, Literary Review*, and *Serving House: A Journal of Literary Arts*. McLean completed her thesis module in 2011 in Fairleigh Dickinson University's MFA Creative Writing Program, Fiction. She is currently working on a short story collection and a novella.

Diane McWhorter has been self-employed for most of her working life, beginning as a traveling sign painter in the early 1970s. She was a finalist in the Oregon Quarterly "Northwest Perspectives" Essay Contest in 2001. She currently blogs at Gelatinaceae@blogspot.com and divinetension@blogspot.com and displays her products at Gelatinaceae.com

Valerie Miner is the author of fourteen books, including the novel, *Traveling*

with Spirits, 2013. Her work has appeared in *The Village Voice, Salmagundi, Ploughshares, The Georgia Review, Prairie Schooner, Gettysburg Review, Southwest Review*, and many other journals. She has won awards and fellowships from The Rockefeller Foundation, the Fulbright Commission, the Jerome Foundation, the Australia Council Literary Arts Board, and various other sources. She is a professor and artist in residence at Stanford University.

Elisabeth Murawski is the author of *Zorba's Daughter*, winner of the 2010 May Swenson Poetry Award, *Moon and Mercury*, and the chapbooks *Troubled by an Angel* and *Out-patients*. She was a Hawthornden fellow in 2008. Her poem "Abu Ghraib Suggests the Isenheim Altarpiece" won the 2006 Ann Stanford Prize. Publications include: *The Yale Review, The Virginia Quarterly Review, FIELD, Southern Review, Ontario Review, The New Republic, The Literary Review*, et al. A native of Chicago, she currently lives in Alexandria, Virginia.

Alicia Ostriker has published thirteen poetry collections, including *The Book of Seventy*, which received the 2009 National Jewish Book Award for Poetry. *The Crack in Everything* and *The Little Space: Poems Selected and New, 1969-1989* were both National Book Award finalists. As a critic, Ostriker has written several books on poetry and on the Bible. Ostriker is Professor Emerita of Rutgers University, and teaches in the Low-Residency Poetry MFA Program of Drew University.

Fax Sinclair started her creative life with acting. After some acting school, a summer at Pasadena Playhouse, and two seasons at A.C.T. in San Francisco, she went to Hollywood. That was it for acting. She fled to the hills of Northern California to become a poet—meanwhile attending Marin Junior College, Santa Rosa Junior College, and Sonoma State. The northward migration continued up to Eugene, Oregon where she was part of Ken Kesey's 2nd Annual Perpetual Poetic Hoo Haw. Fax was invited into Kate Wilhelm and Damon Knight's invitational monthly writing workshop, which she attended for eight years. Also she was accepted to the Clarion Writers Workshop and attended at MSU in 1977. She helped to found The Radar Angels and performed with them at many weird events. She was an Oregon Country Fairy. In 2001 she bought a digital camera while living in Hawaii and an instant photographer was born! She now lives in Mariposa, California, with her cat Graceson (aka The Smudge) but still spends time on the Big Island of Hawaii. Her images can be seen at fax-sinclair.com

Carol Smallwood co-edited (Molly Peacock, foreword) *Women on Poetry: Tips on Writing, Teaching and Publishing by Successful Women Poets* (McFarland, 2012). *Compartments: Poems on Nature, Femininity and Other Realms* (Anaphora Literary Press, 2011) was nominated for the Pushcart Prize. *Women Writing on Family: Tips on Writing, Teaching and Publishing* (Key Publishing House, 2012) is her most recent book. Carol has appeared in *English Journal, Michigan Feminist Studies,* and *The Writer's Chronicle*. Her sixth book for the American Library Association,

Bringing Arts into the Library, is forthcoming. *Lily's Odyssey,* her first novel (All Things That Matter Press, 2010) had its first chapter included in *Best New Writing in Prose 2010. Contemporary American Women: Our Defining Passages,* 2009, is also from All Things That Matter Press. Her first book, for Michigan educators, appeared in 1980.

Laurie Stone is the author of three works of fiction and nonfiction. A longtime writer for the *Village Voice,* she has been theater critic for *The Nation,* critic-at-large on *Fresh Air,* a member of The Bat Theater Company, and a regular writer for *Ms Magazine.* Her numerous memoir essays and stories have appeared in such publications as *Open City, nthWord, TriQuarterly, The Literary Review, Threepenny Review, Speakeasy, Exquisite Corpse, Stone Canoe, American Theatre, Intar Journal, Signs,* and *Creative Nonfiction.* Among other anthologies, her work is included in *They're at it Again: Stories from Twenty Years of Open City, In the Fullness of Time, The Face in the Mirror, The Other Woman,* and *Full Frontal Fiction.* She recently completed *My Life as an Animal: A Memoir* and is at work on *The Pain of Language,* a collection of essays, and *Unmarked Trail: A Romance in Stories* in collaboration with Richard Toon.

Gladys Swan is both a writer and a visual artist. She has published two novels, *Carnival for the Gods* in the Vintage Contemporaries Series, and *Ghost Dance: A Play of Voices,* nominated by LSU Press for the PEN Faulkner and PEN West awards. *News from the Volcano,* a novella and stories, set mostly in New Mexico, was nominated for the PEN/Faulkner Award and the National Book Critics' Circle Award. *The Tiger's Eye: New & Selected Stories* is the most recent of her seven collections of short fiction and has been nominated for a Pulitzer Prize. Her stories have been selected for various anthologies, including *Best of the West.* Her fiction, poetry, and essays have appeared in the *Sewanee Review, Kenyon Review, Virginia Quarterly Review, Chelsea, Ohio Review, New Letters, Southwest Review, Hunger Mountain, Hotel Amerika,* and others. She has received a Lilly Endowment Open Fellowship and a Fulbright Fellowship to Yugoslavia, as well as a Lawrence Foundation Award for fiction and a Tate Prize for poetry.

Susan Tiberghien, an American-born writer living in Switzerland, has published three memoirs, *Looking for Gold, Circling to the Center,* and *Footsteps, A European Album, 1955-1990,* and most recently, *One Year to A Writing Life,* along with numerous narrative essays in journals and anthologies on both sides of the Atlantic. She teaches and lectures at graduate programs, C.G. Jung Centers, for the International Women's Writing Guild, and at writers' conferences both in the United States and in Europe, where she directs the Geneva Writers' Group and Conferences. Her website is www.susantiberghien.com

Ellen Visson is a seven-time nominee for the Pushcart Prize and finalist for the 2007 Eric Hoffer Award, with numerous stories published in such literary magazines as *Pleiades, The Literary Review, The Chattahoochee Review, Ascent,* and *Tiferet,* among others. Ellen lives in Switzerland, where she is completing a third novel. This essay is her second appearance in a Serving House anthology.

Editors

R.A. Rycraft has published stories, poems, essays, reviews, and interviews in a number of journals and anthologies, including *PIF Magazine, VerbSap, Perigee, MacGuffin, Calyx, Contemporary World Literature, Web del Sol,* and *The Absinthe Literary Review.* Winner of the Eric Hoffer Best New Writing Editor's Choice Award for 2008 and a Special Mention for the 2010 Pushcart Prize, Rycraft is chair of the English department at Mt. San Jacinto College in Menifee, California and nonfiction editor at *Serving House: A Journal of Literary Arts.*

Leslie What is a Nebula Award-winning writer and the author of a novel, *Olympic Games,* and two short story collections: *Crazy Love* and *The Sweet and Sour Tongue. Crazy Love* earned starred reviews from *Booklist* and *Publishers Weekly* and was a finalist for the Oregon Book Award. She currently teaches in the Writers' Program at UCLA Extension and is the fiction editor of *Phantom Drift,* a journal of New Fabulism. Her work has been published in a number of anthologies and journals, including *Midstream, Utne Reader, Parabola, Los Angeles Review, Asimov's,* and others.

Acknowledgments

"Approaching Seventy" and "Insomnia" from *The Book of Seventy* by Alicia Suskin Ostriker, © 2009. Reprinted by permission of the University of Pittsburgh Press.

"Blowback" and "The View From Here" were first published in Bette Lynch Husted's poetry collection *At This Distance*, Wordcraft of Oregon, 2010.

"Dark Charms," "Lost in Costco," "Mother's Day," "Over the Hedge," from *The Book of Men* by Dorianne Laux. Copyright © 2011 by Dorianne Laux. Used by permission of W. W. Norton & Company, Inc.

Elisabeth Murawski's "Voyage to the End" appeared in *Elixir* and on *Verse Daily*; "Incense for the Blithe" appeared in *Montserrat Review*; "This Morning in Winter" appeared in *Tiferet* and the Serving House Books chapbook *Out-patients*; "as I grow old" appeared in *Virginia Quarterly Review*; and "The Octogenarians" appeared in *Commonwealth*.

Jan Eliot's "Card-Playing Little Old Ladies," "I Look Like My Mother," "What Waist?" and "Well Seasoned," from the comic strip *Stone Soup*. Copyright © Jan Eliot 2011. Distributed by Universal UClick. All rights reserved. Reprinted with permission.

Kelly Cherry:
"To Catullus—Highet (A reponse to the Highet translation of Catullus 70)," from *Lovers and Agnostics* (published by Red Clay Press, 1975; Carnegie Mellon Contemporary Classics, 1995). "Lines Written on the Eve of a Birthday," published in *Relativity: A Point of View* (L.S.U, 1977; Carnegie Mellon Classic Contemporaries, 2000).

Michelle Bitting's "Patti Smith—after the premiere of 'Dream of Life'" first appeared in *Cortland Review*.

Renée Ashley's "Eighty" from *Salt*, Univ. of Wisconsin Press, Brittingham Prize in Poetry, 1991.

Supriya Bhatnagar's "Memories and Misgivings" first appeared in *NEO 11* and will appear in an anthology by *Drunken Boat*.

Clare MacQueen's "The Fragrance of Levity" was first published in *Serving House: A Journal of Literary Arts*, Issue 4, Fall 2011.

13226119R10133

Made in the USA
Charleston, SC
24 June 2012